EAST AFRICA

KENYA

UGANDA

TANZANIA

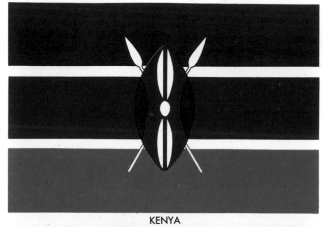

KENYA

UGANDA

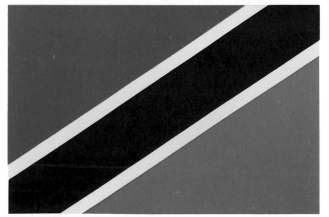

TANZANIA

EAST AFRICA

By the Editors of Time-Life Books

TIME-LIFE BOOKS · AMSTERDAM

TIME-LIFE BOOKS

EUROPEAN EDITOR: Kit van Tulleken
Assistant European Editor: Gillian Moore
Design Director: Ed Skyner
Photography Director: Pamela Marke
Chief of Research: Vanessa Kramer
Chief Sub-Editor: Ilse Gray

LIBRARY OF NATIONS

Series Editor: Tony Allan

Editorial Staff for *East Afrika*
Editors: John Cottrell, John Gaisford
Researcher: Krystyna Mayer
Designer: Lynne Brown
Sub-Editor: Jane Hawker
Picture Co-ordinator: Peggy Tout
Editorial Assistant: Molly Oates

EDITORIAL PRODUCTION

Co-ordinator: Nikki Allen
Assistant: Maureen Kelly
Editorial Department: Theresa John, Debra Lelliott

CONSULTANTS: Basil Davidson is one of the world's foremost authorities on African affairs. He has written more than 30 books on Africa, including *Africa: History of a Continent*, and *Africa in Modern History*, and has been Vice President of the Anti-Apartheid Movement since 1969.

Dr. John Mack is an anthropologist and curator of East African exhibits at the Museum of Mankind, London.

Israel Wamala is Deputy Head of the British Broadcasting Corporation's external service to Africa.

Contributors: The chapter texts were written by: Nicholas Best, Victoria Brittain, Windsor Chorlton, Basil Davidson, Peter Marshall and John Nagenda.

Cover: Zebras browse beneath acacia trees in Tanzania's Tarangire National Park, where the parched plain is dotted with termite mounds.

Front and back endpapers: A topographic map showing the major rivers, lakes, mountain ranges and other natural features of East Africa appears on the front endpaper; the back endpaper shows the three countries of East Africa, with the principal towns and islands.

This volume is one in a series of books describing countries of the world—their natural resources, peoples, histories, economies and governments.

ISBN 7054 0858 2

TIME-LIFE is a trademark of Time Incorporated U.S.A.

CONTENTS

SHARP VARIATIONS IN CLIMATE

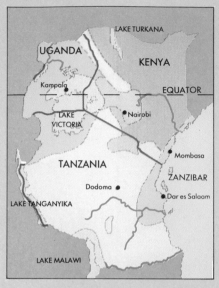

The three countries of East Africa are all situated on or near the equator. Their average temperatures, however, are about 5°C less than those in typical equatorial regions—a reduction largely due to the high altitudes found within the area. Variations in relief also explain huge differences in the average rainfall. More than 70 per cent of Kenya receives so little rain that it is desert or semi-arid; and almost 75 per cent of Tanzania is dry-season savannah—sparse woodland starved of water for six or seven months every year. By contrast, the area around Lake Victoria, including much of Uganda, has seven to 10 months of substantial rainfall that gives rise to a wet-season savannah of tall grassland and broadleaf trees. Heat and humidity, broken by heavy downpours, characterize East Africa's coastal region, while the temperate highlands of Kenya and Tanzania have warm days and cool nights.

	Average rainfall (in mm)	Average temp. (°C)
DESERT AND SEMI-ARID	384	26.3
DRY-SEASON SAVANNAH	890	22.9
HIGHLANDS	1006	19.1
LAKE BASIN	1144	22.8
COASTAL	1153	24.2
RAINY-SEASON SAVANNAH	1161	23.3
SAVANNAH HIGHLAND	1993	21.6

Storm clouds gather over Kenya's offshore island of Lamu. From March to September, moisture-laden airstreams sweep across the Indian Ocean, delivering

heavy showers known as the Long Rains to the islands and coast before reaching the East African interior, where precipitation is much lower.

A DIVERSITY OF BELIEFS

After a century of evangelical activity by European missionaries and African laymen, Christianity is the dominant religion in Kenya and Uganda, where roughly two thirds of the population profess Christian beliefs. The Protestant and Catholic Churches are almost equally represented. In addition, there are numerous local sects, allowing adherence to a wide variety of creeds. In Kenya, for example, almost one in three of the nation's 14 million Christians belongs to one of 200 or so African independent churches. Many of these have split from mission-founded churches within the past few decades to incorporate indigenous beliefs, African customs or revivalist practices.

In Tanzania, where a large section of the population still holds to traditional faiths, religious categories are less clear-cut. Perhaps one in three accepts some form of Christianity. A similar proportion are Muslims, almost all living near the coast or on the offshore islands of Zanzibar and Pemba, where Islam has held sway for over a millennium. The other important minority religion of East Africa is Hindu, the faith of many of the region's Asian communities.

On a road outside the north Kenyan town of Kisumu, a priest of the Legio Maria church struggles to balance a cartload of hay. The Legio Maria (Legion of

Mary) split from the Roman Catholic Church in 1962; now, with some 150,000 members, it is one of the largest of East Africa's independent churches.

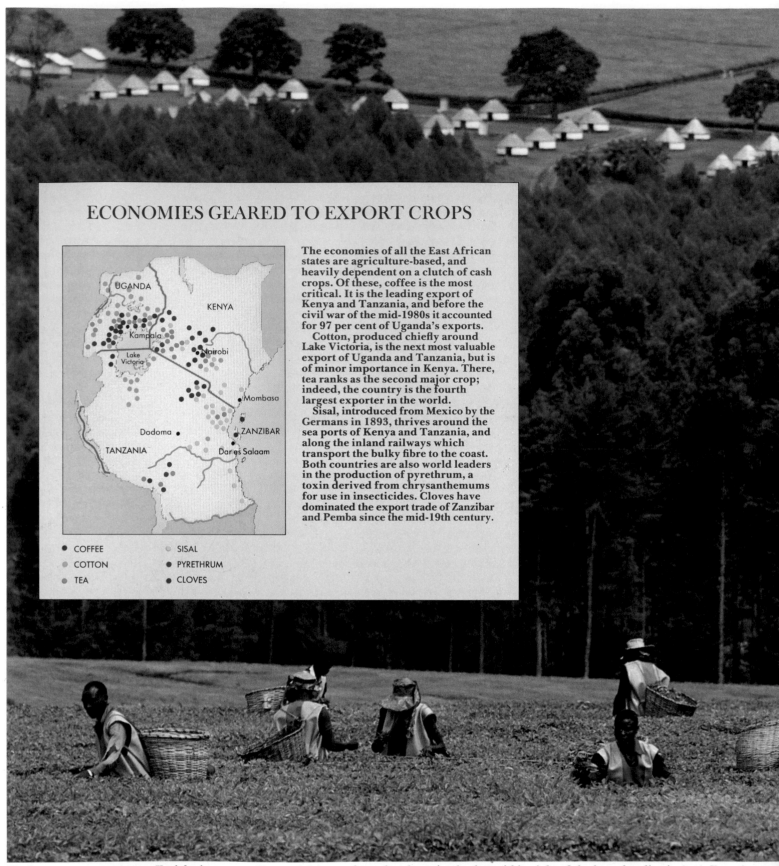

ECONOMIES GEARED TO EXPORT CROPS

The economies of all the East African states are agriculture-based, and heavily dependent on a clutch of cash crops. Of these, coffee is the most critical. It is the leading export of Kenya and Tanzania, and before the civil war of the mid-1980s it accounted for 97 per cent of Uganda's exports.

Cotton, produced chiefly around Lake Victoria, is the next most valuable export of Uganda and Tanzania, but is of minor importance in Kenya. There, tea ranks as the second major crop; indeed, the country is the fourth largest exporter in the world.

Sisal, introduced from Mexico by the Germans in 1893, thrives around the sea ports of Kenya and Tanzania, and along the inland railways which transport the bulky fibre to the coast. Both countries are also world leaders in the production of pyrethrum, a toxin derived from chrysanthemums for use in insecticides. Cloves have dominated the export trade of Zanzibar and Pemba since the mid-19th century.

- ● COFFEE
- ● COTTON
- ● TEA
- ● SISAL
- ● PYRETHRUM
- ● CLOVES

Workers on a tea estate near Kericho in western Kenya pick leaves from the plantation bushes within sight of the huts they live in *(top)*. Kenya's tea

production in the mid-1980s amounted to 147,000 tonnes, accounting for over a quarter of the country's total foreign earnings.

CROWDED ZONES IN EMPTY SPACES

Throughout East Africa, rainfall is the key to human settlement patterns. For the region as a whole, the population density is a modest 28 people per square kilometre; but where the land is fertile and well watered, the figure rises to as many as 400 per square kilometre. The chief clusters, as shown on the map below, are around Lake Victoria and in the Kenya Highlands to the east, where good precipitation encourages arable farming and the dry season is not too harsh. In contrast, there are enormous areas—notably the desert land of northern Kenya and the semi-arid, tsetse fly-infested savannah of much of Tanzania—that are almost totally shunned by humans.

East Africa remains a region of farmers and pastoralists, with over 90 per cent of the population dwelling in rural areas. But the high birth rate, increasing the headcount by more than 3 per cent a year, is putting severe pressure on the fertile areas and has accelerated the drift to the cities. The fastest-growing centres are Nairobi, Kampala and Dar es Salaam, which between them house 2.5 million inhabitants—roughly half the entire urban population of the region.

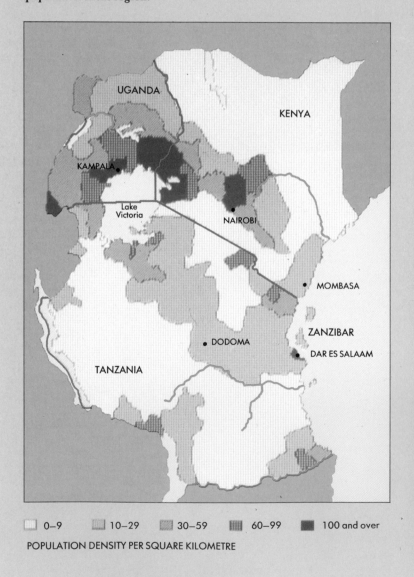

POPULATION DENSITY PER SQUARE KILOMETRE

Legend: 0–9 | 10–29 | 30–59 | 60–99 | 100 and over

Brightly dressed women stroll down a roadway in Dar es Salaam. With more than 700,000 inhabitants, Dar is Tanzania's only major city.

13

Giraffes browsing on thorn trees in Kenya's Great Rift Valley are dwarfed by the immense dishes of the Longonot Earth Station near Naivasha. Built

14

by a British company and inaugurated in 1970, it is used for a wide range of telecommunication purposes, including TV reception and transmission.

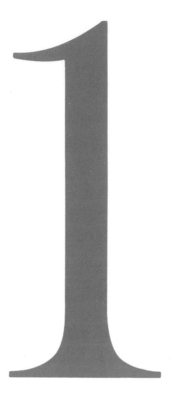

Fishing dhows, silhouetted against the shimmering sun, work the coastal waters of Lake Victoria off the Kenyan port of Kisumu. Kenya, Tanzania and Uganda converge on the shores of the lake—an inland sea that affords them valuable food and an important means of intercommunication.

WHERE MAN BEGAN

Nature has fashioned East Africa on a most lavish scale, endowing it with scenery of epic proportions and kaleidoscopic contrasts. Sprawling across equatorial latitudes which elsewhere are characterized by a green, leafy sameness, this is a land of unique variety, encompassing tropical woodlands and permanent snowfields, dusty plains and mangrove swamps, active volcanoes and thundering waterfalls. It includes snow-capped Kilimanjaro, Africa's summit and the highest free-standing mountain in the world; Victoria, the world's second largest freshwater lake and the source of its longest river, the Nile; and, most dramatically, a vast section of the Great Rift Valley, a fissure in the earth's crust so large that it is visible from outer space.

Over the face of this land moves the greatest concentration of game animals on the earth—millions of zebras, wildebeest, buffaloes, elephants, antelopes and giraffes, attended by carnivores such as lions, leopards, cheetahs, hyenas and hunting dogs. Here, too, for millennia man has made his home, adapting his way of life to fit the varied contours of nature, with the result that the region's 56 million inhabitants, divided into more than 200 tribes and peoples, represent an extraordinary cross section of lifestyles, social behaviour and cultural traditions.

As a geographical entity, East Africa is fairly clearly defined. The greater part of its land area consists of a vast plateau bounded to the east by the Indian Ocean, to the west by the rainforests of Zaire, to the north by the deserts and highlands of the Sudan and Ethiopia, and to the south by the deep trench of Lake Malawi (formerly Lake Nyasa) and the virtually uninhabited savannah country along the Ruvuma river which marks the border with Mozambique. Within these boundaries there are three contrasting independent states: Kenya and Uganda in the north, and in the south, Tanzania—formed by the union of mainland Tanganyika with the offshore islands of Zanzibar, Mafia and Pemba.

Tanzania is the largest, most populous and multi-tribal of the three countries. It covers almost 1 million square kilometres, inhabited by about 21 million people belonging to perhaps 120 ethnic communities. Kenya is little more than half the size of Tanzania, though it is fast closing on its southern neighbour in terms of population, sheltering 20 million inhabitants in the mid-1980s. Uganda, at 235,000 square kilometres, is the smallest East African country, but is also the most densely populated, with just under 15 million inhabitants. All three states are essentially agricultural economies and are bonded together by language. Swahili, the official language of Kenya and Tanzania, is widely spoken in Uganda; and English, the official language of Uganda, is commonly spoken in Kenya and Tanzania.

As a political entity, East Africa is much less clearly defined. In this respect, the only common feature shared by the three nations is their experience of European colonial rule. The Germans administered Tanganyika from

1

1890 until 1918, while the British colonized Kenya (then known as British East Africa) from the 1880s onwards, and administered all three countries from the end of World War I until the 1960s. As a legacy of colonization, all three countries remain members of the Commonwealth, a 49-strong voluntary association of nations who meet every two years to consider a variety of international issues, and whose only common denominator is that they were once ruled by Britain.

After gaining independence in the early 1960s, the countries made attempts to forge closer links with one another, most notably by way of the Treaty of East African Co-operation, which was signed in 1967 with high hopes of creating a free trade area and pooling scarce resources to promote economic growth. However, again and again, their efforts to advance unity foundered; and by 1977, when Kenya seized control of the jointly owned East African Airways, the last vestiges of the three countries' alliance had been completely destroyed.

The dream of union was made impossible because each country chose to follow a different political path. Tanzania has attempted to build itself a socialist, egalitarian republic based on an agrarian revolution, self-reliance and the nationalization of key industries and banks. Kenya, which unlike Tanzania and Uganda began Independence with a sizeable population of colonial white settlers, has retained strong links with the West by encouraging foreign investment and building a mixed economy. Uganda, one of the most fertile regions in the continent, has been plunged into political and economic anarchy under a succession of despotic rulers—most infamously,

by the unstable and brutal rule of the dictator Idi Amin.

"Tribalism" has often been blamed for the ills that have beset and divided the East African countries, and undoubtedly the heterogeneous nature of the region's society has been a major obstacle to administration on a national scale. Prior to colonial rule, Uganda had a relatively organized society, being dominated by four centralized feudal kingdoms in which small aristocracies were served by a majority of peasants. In Kenya and Tanganyika, however, a multitude of different groups existed independently of one another; most of them did not even have chiefs and were content to leave the day-to-day decisions in the hands of local elders.

Development of national identities was indirectly encouraged by colonial rule which established the borders between the East African countries—frontiers which were to become so firmly established in administrative usage that they have prevailed to the present day. At the same time, the drawing of the borders often had a divisive effect. They were arbitrary creations, which lumped together peoples of different cultures and lifestyles on the one hand, and cut through social groups with traditional affinities on the other. It is little wonder that Kenya, Uganda and Tanzania—only recently exposed to the concept of nationhood and bound together internally by no traditions of unity—have encountered enormous socio-economic problems since gaining independence.

Underlying the social complexity of East Africa is the complexity of the physical environment and climate. In many areas, difficult terrain restricts communications between the various tribal groups, and dramatically variable climatic conditions have given rise to uneven settlement and land development. Basically, the region is a huge plateau that rises from a narrow coastal belt to a general altitude of between 1,000 and 2,000 metres—high enough to make evening fires welcome in the upland communities, even though the line of the equator crosses the northern half of the territory.

The most imposing feature of the whole plateau is the Great Rift Valley, a 6,500-kilometre-long fissure which splits the earth's crust from the Lebanon in the north to Mozambique. The rift—a steep-sided trench almost 60 kilometres across and 2,000 metres deep—enters East Africa at Kenya's Lake Turkana. It then rises to Lake Naivasha, the highest lake in the valley, and runs almost due south through part of Tanzania before petering out beyond Lake Malawi. From this main trunk, another fissure branches out at Lake Malawi, curving north-west to form a natural frontier between the East African plateau and the rainforests of the Zaire basin.

Geologists believe that some of the main faulting of the East African rift valley occurred long after the first appearance of man in the region. Tectonic forces created it by causing huge chunks of the earth's crust to sink downwards; and those same forces drove up molten rock that buried the ancient surface of the plateau under volcanic highlands. On the northern border of Tanzania, three separate volcanoes coalesced to form Mount Kilimanjaro, which only stopped growing about 100,000 years ago. Rising in solitary grandeur from a plain that is only three degrees south of the equator, the

snow-capped dome of the mountain reaches 5,896 metres, so that a climber who makes the ascent (a feasible proposition for any reasonably fit person) passes from tropical to arctic conditions in the space of only three to four days' travel.

Three hundred kilometres north of Kilimanjaro, and visible from its summit on a clear day, is Mount Kenya, Africa's second highest peak, which soars 5,199 metres above the surround-ing plain. If anything, it is even more beautiful than Tanzania's crown. An early European explorer described it as "a gleaming snow-white peak with sparkling facets which scintillated with the superb beauty of a colossal dia-mond". The scenic contrasts are no less striking than those of its southern rival: low-lying farmlands and savan-nah give way on its flanks to bamboo jungle and dense forests, moors and valleys, trout-rich rivers, lakes, gla-ciers and, finally, icy towers presenting breathtaking views of much of Kenya.

The third great isolated peak of East Africa is Mount Elgon, a 4,321-metre-high colossus bestriding the Kenya-Uganda border. Rising gently from the Kenyan side, it dominates the low plains of eastern Uganda and has a volcanic crater more than 6 kilometres in diameter. However, the most spec-tacular mountains in Uganda belong to the Ruwenzori range, the only East

KARAMOJONG (Uganda)

KIKUYU (Kenya)

BONI (Kenya)

Acholi
Jie
Lango
Karamojong
Turkana
Gabbra
Chope
Teso
Rendille
Nyoro
Pokot
Somali
Ganda
Toro
KAMPALA
Luyia
Samburu
Ankole
Nandi
Kikuyu
Meru
UGANDA
Kipsigis
Embu
Luo
Kamba
LAKE
VICTORIA
Kisii
NAIROBI
KENYA
Kuria
Galla
Boni
Masai
Haya
Mijikenda
Zinza
Sukuma
Chagga
Taita
MOMBASA
Ha
Hadza
Pare
Nyamwezi
Iraqw
Sandawe
Shamba
Iramba
Nguru
TANZANIA
Gogo
Luguru
Shirazi
DODOMA
ZANZIBAR
Kaguru
Fipa
Sangu
Hehe
Sagara
Zaramo
DAR ES SALAAM
Nyakyusa
Ngoni
Yao
Makonde

SOMALI (Kenya)

SAMBURU (Kenya)

GABBRA (Kenya)

KIPSIGIS (Kenya)

GANDA (Uganda)

MASAI (Kenya and Tanzania)

MAKONDE (Tanzania)

SHIRAZI (Zanzibar)

A MOSAIC OF PEOPLES

A complex mosaic of peoples inhabit East Africa, each with their own language and traditions. Some of the groups number only a few hundred, but others are considerable: Tanzania boasts 100 communities of 10,000 or more. The map *(opposite)* locates the most notable groups, including the two biggest, the Kikuyu and the Ganda, whose numbers both exceed 3,000,000.

As the accompanying portraits here show, many of the peoples wear distinctive costumes. The women of the Masai of Kenya and Tanzania wear elaborate necklaces made of row upon row of beads; in Uganda, Karamojong men pack their hair with painted clay to form a decorative headdress; and the Somali women of northern Kenya cover their heads with shawls. Traditional costume is less common in the capital cities, where most people have adopted some form of Western dress.

Broadly, the peoples of the region divide into two main groups, the Bantu and the Nilotics. The Bantu, including the Kikuyu and Ganda, form the overwhelming majority of East Africa's population: their ancestors were farmers who came originally from the west and settled wherever land was suitable for agriculture. The ancestors of the Nilotics were cattle-herders from the north; like the Kipsigis and the Masai, they moved south along the Great Rift Valley, grazing their herds on the open plains.

The distinctions are blurring now as lifestyles change, but they still exert a lingering influence. Rivalries between peoples of Bantu and of Nilotic origin helped to inflame the 1985–86 civil war in Uganda, while in Kenya and Tanzania Nilotic cattle-herders like the Rendille *(page 148)* have resisted the encroachment of modern life.

African heights that are not of volcanic origin. More than 80 kilometres in length, with 10 of the peaks topping 4,500 metres, the range was formed by upfaulting and warping which produced a convoluted massif known to the ancients as the "Mountains of the Moon". Further south, the Virunga Mountains—active volcanoes which have staged several eruptions during the present century—extend along the borders of Uganda, Rwanda and Zaire. The thick bamboo forests which cover their lower slopes are the home of the only surviving mountain gorillas in the world.

Altogether, some 30 East African volcanoes still show signs of activity. They include Ol Doinyo Lengai, "the mountain of God", which stands by itself in the Great Rift Valley close to Tanzania's northern border. In 1983, the mountain relieved some of the pressures still at work under the rift by blowing up, and in the process coated its 610-metre cone with an alkaline lava which, on contact with the air, immediately turned to crystals of sodium carbonate—washing soda.

However, the great majority of East Africa's volcanoes are long dead, their centres collapsed inward by the sudden withdrawal of molten lava. The most spectacular example of such collapse is Ngorongoro, just west of Ol Doinyo Lengai. It represents one of the world's greatest natural wonders: the largest crater in Africa, with a floor covering an area of more than 250 square kilometres. Its unbroken 610-metre-high walls rise to a forest-clad rim frequently cloaked in mists that perhaps inspired the region's local name, which translated means "Cold Place". On the floor of this tremendous amphitheatre, the forest gives way to

rolling savannah, which supports vast herds of wildebeest, zebra, gazelle and buffalo, and all their predators.

Another distinctive feature of East Africa's topography is the prodigious size of its lakes, some so enormous that they were described by early explorers as "inland seas". Lake Victoria, for example, is an irregular quadrilateral of shallow water that fills a depression about the size of Scotland. Bordered by all three East African countries, and lying at the headwaters of the White Nile, it is a storage reservoir for much of the continent, as well as being a rich source of fish for the densely populated settlements on its margins.

In complete contrast, Lake Tanganyika on Tanzania's western border is serpentine and deep—675 kilometres long, on average less than 50 kilometres wide and in parts more than 1,400 metres deep. Indeed, it is the second deepest freshwater lake in the world, surpassed only by Lake Baikal in Siberia in the Soviet Union. It is also the richest lake for fish, with more than 250 different species, including tiger fish, yellow-bellies, Nile perch and the prolific *dagga*, a small sardine-like fish that is sun-dried and distributed throughout Tanzania, where it is a dietary staple.

Beyond the mountains and lakes, the greater part of East Africa may be divided into four categories of terrain: open bushland, savannah, well-watered highlands and semi-desert or desert. The contrasting vegetation cover of each area reflects the enormous variations in rainfall.

In broad terms, the areas around the equator have two wet seasons every year—from March to May and from November to December. In the most arid areas to the north, the rains may

1

be confined to April alone, while in arid zones to the south there are only two short rainy periods—in April and December. Unfortunately, however, there are many areas where the rainfall cannot be predicted. In northern Kenya, for example, the rainy season may fail completely. This occurred dramatically in 1961 when a prolonged drought resulted in the death of thousands of animals. Then, unexpectedly, came floods in which many more animals drowned. Conversely, parts of the Lake Victoria Basin, a fertile crescent of land extending from Mount Elgon to the Masaka region near the Tanzanian border, receive so much rain that it is often difficult to distinguish one wet season from another.

Not surprisingly, the greatest population densities tend to coincide with the fertile areas of relatively high rainfall: in Kenya, the coast and central highlands; in Uganda, the south-west highlands; in Tanzania, the southern highlands and the land around Kilimanjaro; and the territory shared between all three countries along the shores of Lake Victoria. The number of livestock is also greatest in these well-watered areas, but they form only one component of an economy that is chiefly dependent on cash crops such as tea, coffee and cotton. In the third of East Africa's territory that receives less than 500 millimetres of rainfall every year, however, livestock are virtually the sole basis of life for pastoralists herding cattle, goats and camels.

Over large tracts of East Africa, though, neither man nor livestock are present in appreciable numbers—not because the areas are too dry, but simply because they are infested by an insect only a trifle larger than the common housefly. This is the tsetse fly, a

Clouds swirl round one of several peaks on Mount Kenya, the highest point in Kenya. Lying on the equator, the 5,199-metre mountain is an extinct volcano whose crater has been completely stripped away by erosion to expose the resistant plugs of lava that form its jagged heights.

In Tanzania, a sunlit grove of acacia trees glows against the shadowed rim of Ngorongoro, Africa's largest intact volcanic crater. Its floor—more than 250 square kilometres of woodland and grass—supports one of the heaviest concentrations of wildlife in Africa.

brownish pest with a few yellow stripes or spots underneath, which takes its name from the peculiar hissing sound it makes. Living only on the blood of mammals, which it sucks after piercing the skin, it has a bite no worse than that of a mosquito. Unfortunately, in the process of feeding, the fly often ingests microscopic single-celled organisms called trypanosomes, some of which, after being passed on, cause sleeping sickness, a debilitating disease that can prove fatal both to man and, more especially, to his domestic animals, but to which wild animals are curiously immune. Despite intensive bush clearing and the spraying of new insecticides in suitable areas, the little pest represents the greatest natural impediment to man's prosperity in East Africa. It has managed to render inhospitable two thirds of mainland Tanzania, one third of Uganda and about one tenth of Kenya.

The tsetse fly requires shade as well as blood, and therefore its favourite habitat is the so-called *miombo*— woodland that is occupied by little except wildlife and composed of a light canopy of moderate-sized, well-spaced trees standing in a thin ground cover of grasses. Consequently, the *miombo*— land that is most extensive in the western plateau of Tanzania—is the most unproductive human environment in the region. It supports only a few hardy slash-and-burn farmers and a small number of scattered communities of honey-gatherers, people who make a modest living with the aid of that remarkable African bird, the black-throated honey-guide.

This bird, which boasts the Latin name of *Indicator-indicator*, can locate honey but cannot extract it unaided. Long ago, it evolved a symbiotic part-nership with man—by making a particular cry to hunters and then, very deliberately, flying off and circling a honey tree until the gatherers arrive to cut open the concealed hive. After fulfilling its mission, the bird then waits patiently to feast upon the leavings of man's raid. If no honey is left for the feathered guide, Africans say, the bird will lead the next honey-seeker to a snake or a lion.

Infested by tsetse flies, waterless for half the year, and with soils leached of nutrients by the seasonal rains, the *miombo* might seem as unappealing a place as the dark side of the moon. Yet, every year, this wooded bushland (and other more open country) is visited by hundreds of thousands of foreign tourists. Riding in air-conditioned cars and coaches and well equipped with pest-repellents, visitors flock to these wilderness areas because they are the main refuge of East Africa's extra-ordinary wildlife. Since more than 50 species of the region's wild animals are hosts of the sleeping sickness parasites, game destruction was once seen as the most effective means of waging war on the disease transmitted by the tsetse fly. But not any more. Such is the commercial importance of tourism that all of the East African countries have designated large tracts of their land as game parks and reserves. In Kenya, for example, tourism now accounts for about 20 per cent of all its foreign currency earnings.

In size, these areas range from the 115 square kilometres of Nairobi National Park—about twice the size of Manhattan—where tourists can photograph lions and giraffes against a city skyline, to the huge Selous Game Reserve in south-east Tanzania, where more than 100,000 elephants, 150,000 buffaloes and about 2,000 rhinos roam an area about the size of the Republic

23

1

A gaggle of hornbills and smaller birds seek crumbs from the tables of tourists at Kilaguni Lodge in Tsavo National Park, Kenya's largest game reserve. The lodge overlooks two water holes which are floodlit at night to enable visitors to watch elephants, lions and other big game feeding.

of Ireland. Since some of the animals in the Selous have to be culled to prevent the population spreading into inhabited areas nearby, the Tanzanian Wildlife Corporation grants hunters the dubious privilege of killing a quota of the world's largest mammals for a suitably mammoth price. A month's elephant safari, for example, can cost as much as a small car—excluding such items as game licences (nearly £2,500 per kill in the case of elephants) and the expense of mounting and stuffing the trophies.

Established as a game reserve by the Germans in 1905, the Selous is the most remote and the largest wildlife sanctuary in the world. Ironically, it perpetuates the name of Captain Frederick Courtney Selous, a British soldier, explorer, naturalist and hunter who personally killed nearly 1,000 head of big game in the region before he was gunned down by enemy soldiers during World War I.

Despite the Selous Reserve's size, the best known and most scientifically important wildlife sanctuary is undoubtedly the Serengeti of northern Tanzania. The highest concentration of game animals on earth is to be found here, including more than two million wildebeest and a quarter of a million zebras which together form the main cast of one of the most spectacular shows in nature—the annual Serengeti migration.

The migration serves as pasture rotation for the grazing animals which congregate on the park's open plains from November to May. Towards the end of that period, when the grass is dry and exhausted, wildebeest mass in their hundreds of thousands, grunting, leaping and bucking, because this is the onset of the breeding season. Suddenly, a pair will break away to the horizon, soon followed by the rest of the herd; and though this may only be a feint, to be repeated many more times, eventually the whole herd will keep moving, six or seven abreast, until they are lost in the distance and their own dust. In the living stream, often several kilometres long, there will also be thousands of zebras, maintaining their own family units and adding their own yelping bark to the sullen grunting of the wildebeest. And in the wake of the grazing animals will come lions, hunting dogs and hyenas, while more predators lie in wait along the line of the great procession.

In the course of this mass migration, thousands of wildebeest and zebras are killed by predators; thousands more are trampled to death or drowned as they stampede across rivers, drawing vultures to the scene like flies. Yet their numbers never seem to be significantly diminished. The herds stream on, at first heading west and then, by some uncanny instinct, separating into two groups—one continuing west before turning north-east, the other heading due north. Finally, after several days' travelling, the groups merge and come to a halt in the area of the Masai Mara Reserve, across the Kenyan border. There they stay until November, when they wheel southwards, heading back to the central plains, drawn by the growth of new grass and the instincts embedded in their species for more than a million years.

East Africa's remarkably prolific and varied animal life can largely be explained by its position astride the equator. This made the region less vulnerable to the violent climatic oscillations of the Ice Ages which, from about

Immobile on their arid grazing lands near the Kenya-Tanzania border, Masai warriors watch the silent passage of a hot-air balloon carrying tourists on a one-hour trip over the Masai Mara game reserve, which has the greatest assembly of predators in Africa.

three million years ago, wiped out much of the fauna living in high latitudes. At the same time, the slight cooling and drying of the region encouraged the growth of grasslands at the expense of tropical forests, and so provided greater space for the development of mass animal populations—including, most significantly, ape-like creatures believed to be the predecessors of modern man.

These proto-humans were not as fleet of foot as the zebras and other grazing animals that emerged on the East African plains, and they had neither sharp teeth nor claws to defend themselves against leopards and lions. But during their earlier existence as forest dwellers, they had probably developed excellent colour vision and depth perception that far exceeded the capacities of the other emerging grassland species; and their hands, evolved for gripping hold of branches, would have proved to be just as well suited to the fashioning and using of both tools and weapons once they had developed the upright posture.

The idea that Africa had been the cradle of mankind was suggested by Charles Darwin in 1871. But it was not until 1959 that the extreme antiquity of our predecessors on the African continent began to be fully appreciated. A major breakthrough was made in July of that year when Mary Leakey, the wife and colleague of the distinguished British anthropologist Doctor Louis Leakey, found two large teeth and a piece of skull in Olduvai Gorge, a dry river gulch about 100 metres deep which cuts across the Serengeti Plain in northern Tanzania.

For more than a quarter of a century, the Leakeys had worked off and on at Olduvai Gorge, recording an enormous number of animal fossils and extremely primitive stone tools. But none of their earlier finds compared with this discovery, made in one of the tributaries to the main gorge. It sent Mary Leakey running back to the camp where her husband lay in his tent sick with fever. "I've got him! I've got him!" she shouted. And so it proved. Subsequently, the Leakeys uncovered more than 400 fragments of bone which enabled them to reconstruct an adult man-like skull. Radiometric dating of the site of the discovery gave an age of 1.7 million years.

One year later, on the same site but at a slightly lower level, the Leakeys found a skull of roughly the same age. This one, however, was even closer to modern man, with smaller teeth and a slightly larger brain than the earlier skull. Its owner was not, Dr. Leakey felt, a man-ape, but sufficiently human to merit classification as a species in our own genus, *Homo*. He christened this find *Homo habilis*, or "Handy Man", believing him to be a direct tool-using ancestor of today's *Homo sapiens*. The Leakeys went on to collect from Olduvai a series of *habilis* fragments, indicating that this type lived there for more than half a million years, using much the same primitive tool culture for the entire time.

A still clearer picture of man-like creatures in prehistoric East Africa came to light in 1984 when a leading Kenyan fossil-hunter called Kamoya Kimeu discovered a small piece of hominoid skull on the west shore of Lake Turkana. Subsequent excavations uncovered an almost complete skeleton, lying on volcanic tuff 1.6 million years old. Analysis showed the body to be that of a young male, aged about 12 and 1.63 metres tall; and it proved to

Near Tsavo National Park, the Chyulu Range stretches to a misty horizon. The hills are made up of hundreds of grass-covered cones of volcanic cinder, which attract heavy rainfall and dew like a sponge, daily feeding the nearby Mzima oasis with over 200 million litres of crystal-clear water.

On an afternoon in January at the end of the two-month wet season, a woman of the pastoral Samburu people crosses scrubland to fill her gourd at a water hole. The Samburu, who subsist mainly on their cattle, are nomadic, frequently moving camp in the dry months in search of fresh watering places.

be the most detailed remains of an early human ever found.

This discovery provided definitive evidence of the size and anatomy of *Homo erectus*, a species intermediate between the first upright-walking hominoids and modern man. Possessing a larger brain than *Homo habilis*, this species made tools and built shelters, hunted animals and spread throughout Africa, Asia and possibly northern Europe, before finally evolving into the modern species, *Homo sapiens*, perhaps 300,000 years ago.

The anthropological trail from such examples of early man to the present inhabitants of the African continent has been erased. Indeed, tracing the origins of East Africa's 200 or more tribal groups is virtually impossible because the region's position astride the corridor of the Great Rift Valley made it a continental crossroads. For thousands of years it was a melting-pot where peoples assimilated, or were assimilated by, other indigenous groups or immigrants, sometimes changing their way of life in the process. There is no written record and archaeological evidence is scanty, so the only clue to a group's origins lies in the linguistic affinities that it may share with peoples who are hundreds, sometimes thousands, of kilometres distant.

There are several main linguistic groups to be found in East Africa. The most important by far is Bantu, a tongue introduced to the region more than a thousand years ago by peoples who filtered in from the west and brought with them a knowledge of iron-working. All three East African countries now have a predominantly Bantu population. In Kenya, Bantu-speaking groups include the Luyia in the west and the Kamba in the centre, each numbering well over two million, and also the country's largest ethnic community, the Kikuyu, roughly four million strong, who are concentrated in the central highlands.

In Uganda, the Bantu speakers are mainly found in the southern half of the country where, in the 14th and the 15th centuries, four kingdoms emerged: Bunyoro, Buganda, Ankole and Toro. Eventually, Buganda became the most powerful of the kingdoms and its people, the Ganda, the largest ethnic group, a position that they still hold today. In Tanzania, too, the people of Bantu origins are in the huge majority. But here, in contrast to Kenya and Uganda, no single group is dominant. The population is divided into about 120 different groups with much less numerical disparity between them. Only the Sukuma number more than one million, and it requires the 14 largest groups to aggregate more than 50 per cent of the total population.

The most prominent of the other main language categories is Nilotic—so-called because of a presumed provenance around the Nile in what is now the Sudan. The majority of the pastoralist groups in East Africa speak languages of the Nilotic class—among them the 250,000 Masai, who live in the grasslands straddling Kenya and Tanzania, and were once renowned as the most fearsome and the best-disci-plined warriors of their region. Other groups in this language category include the Alur and the Acholi of northern Uganda, the Turkana of northern Kenya and the Luo on the eastern shores of Lake Victoria. The Luo, however, differ fundamentally from the majority of Nilotic speakers. They are predominantly farmers and fishermen; and their settled way of life has encouraged a surge in population (now more than 2.5 million), making them one of Kenya's largest tribal groups and the most serious political rivals of the dominant group, Kikuyu.

Since the East African interior was not scientifically explored until the 19th century, little is known about the early history of these tribal groups. In contrast, the development of the coastal region can be traced in some detail from around the eighth century, when Arab merchant-venturers arrived to establish a flourishing trade in gold, ivory and tortoiseshell. As early as A.D. 956 an important book about the East African coast was published in Cairo; written by the renowned Arab geographer Abul-Hasan al Mas'udi, it described the great trading wealth of the land of the *Zanj* ("blacks")—a name that lives on in Zanzibar, literally meaning "Coast of the Blacks". A few decades later, the *Arabian Nights*, a collection of travellers' tales composed in Baghdad, included stories of Sinbad the Sailor that are deeply evocative of early voyages to the island and mainland ports of East Africa.

Sinbad was a character of legend, but his ports of call were all based on fact; they were the real and thriving harbours of a new and burgeoning civilization on the coastal fringe of the continent. Having established trading ports on the mainland and on offshore islands, many Arab immigrants inter-married with native inhabitants. Their descendants were to become known as the Swahili (from *suahil*, the Arabic word for coastland).

The emergent Swahili civilization grew especially prosperous from the late 10th century, when thriving great city-ports, inspired by the architectural splendours of Cairo and Baghdad, began to take shape. Eventually there were more than 40, including Malindi, Mombasa and ports on the three off-shore islands of Zanzibar, Pemba and Mafia. Swahili urban development reached its climax with Kilwa Kisi-wani, "Kilwa-on-the-island", set in a great enclosed bay in southern Tanzania. By the 12th century, Kilwa had developed into a mercantile and military power capable of dominating East Africa's long-distance trade. Its Great Mosque was the largest on the coast and arguably the most beautiful, with its rows of dressed coral pillars, square bays and great domes. Not far away was the largest pre-European building of equatorial Africa, the Husuni Kub-wa, a palace that was built on the spur of a cliff. Covering nearly one hectare, it had more than a hundred rooms, several inner courtyards and a large octagonal outdoor swimming pool, ideally positioned to catch the cool ocean breezes.

With their own Bantu language enriched with borrowings from Arabic, the Swahili played an indispensable role as intermediaries between the gold and ivory producers of the East African interior and traders who came from Arabia and from as far as India, Ceylon and China. Their principal imports were cottons, porcelain, pottery and glass beads; indeed, to this day, along the beach at Kilwa, one may still

Three unladen donkeys make their way along one of the ancient, narrow lanes on the offshore island of Lamu. Motor vehicles are not allowed on the island, and the mule and cart remains the most common form of transport.

chance to pick up fragments of Chinese porcelain or of the fine pottery of medieval Persia and Iraq.

The Swahili's trade with the Chinese was a relatively late development, one arising mainly in the early 15th century during China's brief period of far-ranging maritime exploration. Most especially, this trade was spurred in 1414 by the sensational arrival at the Chinese court of an East African giraffe—a gift from the Swahili city of Malindi to the reigning emperor of the Ming dynasty. In 1417, when a second giraffe arrived, the emperor was so delighted that he ordered the assembly of a full-scale fleet under the command of the eunuch admiral Zheng He to escort the Malindi ambassadors home.

This was a time when China led the world in gigantic ocean craft. Some of Zheng He's junks were more than 100 metres in length, with four decks and watertight compartments. Such a display of power had the desired effect as, at each new port of call, the admiral made known his emperor's desire for tribute. As a result of this voyage and of other high-seas expeditions led by Zheng He, China received tribute-bearing delegates from 36 countries in the Far and Middle East.

But then, quite suddenly, the great age of Chinese seafaring came to an end. A powerful faction at the court in Peking successfully argued the case for isolationism; a new law forbade all ocean-sailing for whatever purpose, and the building of high-seas vessels became a capital offence. By a strange twist of fate, China's new, inward-directed policy coincided with the ever-increasing expansionism of other great seafaring peoples, most notably the Portuguese, Spanish, Dutch and British, who were to intervene much more directly in the affairs of East African countries. In 1498, the Portuguese became the first Europeans to reach the coast. Their arrival was to have a devastating impact on the Swahili civilization, because domination by these autocratic newcomers soon set in motion a rapid, unreversed decline in the Swahili's lucrative Far East trade.

Today, the architectural brilliance of the lost Swahili culture can be perceived only vaguely in the many dusty ruins up and down the coast. But a rich tapestry of its mythology survives in the shape of legends, songs and proverbs that have been passed down by poets, storytellers and scholars. The past lives on, too, in the way of life of the coastal peoples of Kenya and Tanzania. As in the days when the Swahili civilization flourished, many of those living outside the major ports still inhabit rectangular houses of coral, or wattle and daub, with thatched ridged roofs made from coconut fronds. When fishing for horse mackerel, kingfish, tunny, sardines, barracuda and shark, they still sail small *mashua* dhows or the humble *ngalawa*, a small dug-out canoe equipped with an outrigger float borrowed from Indonesian mariners 15 centuries ago. And trading along the coast are a few merchants who still use the ancient *jahazi* dhow, a Swahili ship that is capable of carrying up to 50 tonnes of cargo.

Similarly, some of the sights and sounds of the original Swahili city-ports can now be recognized in their present-day successors. To be sure, the island-city of Mombasa now has a modern side sprawling on to the adjacent mainland; but the Old Town, with its labyrinth of narrow alleyways, remains much as it was in medieval times. The muezzin call the faithful

White Kenyans relax at the race meeting held every Sunday afternoon at Nairobi's Ngong racecourse. Kenya has some 40,000 citizens of European—mainly British—descent, who mostly remain loyal to such old colonial pleasures as cricket, polo, golf, tennis and fishing.

to prayer from the minarets of the mosques, and the harbour is still crowded with dhows—small coastal vessels from Lamu and Mogadishu, and larger boats from the Persian Gulf, sailing in on the monsoon winds.

Likewise, despite visible signs of modernity, the island of Zanzibar contains memories of its great past in its ancient ruins, crumbling amongst coconut and clove plantations. Its capital, the only fully functioning historical town in East Africa, is a maze of dark, tightly grouped streets which can suddenly open out on to dazzling sunlit squares. Here, the wealth of the merchants of long ago is reflected in old coral-stone houses, two or three storeys high, with elaborately carved doors, ornate balconies and inner courtyards that are still the focus of domestic family life. Along the seafront, a chain of

historic palaces bears witness to the luxury and immense power of the sultans in centuries past.

Although its population is one of the most cosmopolitan in the region, Zanzibar retains a timeless quality all of its own. Street traders still cry their wares as they did in medieval times; and in the open workshops carpenters fashion furniture or Zanzibar chests from teak, camphor and cedar, just as their ancestors did generations before them. A sense of history is pervasive even amid the hustle and bustle of the bazaars, where men wear long white robes and embroidered skullcaps, and women, sometimes with henna-painted hands and feet, shift their black over-gowns and reveal their brightly coloured dresses underneath.

Besides the Swahili language, which eventually became the *lingua franca* of

1

all East Africa, the most significant legacy of early Arab settlement is the Islamic religion. For a thousand years it was confined to the coastal communities, but in the 19th century it began to spread along the trade routes into the interior. Today, Islam is the religion of about one third of the population of Tanzania, 3.8 per cent of Kenya and 5 per cent of Uganda. Predictably it has its most ardent following on the coastal strip where it was introduced within a hundred years of the death of the prophet Muhammad.

Asians comprise a significant proportion of East Africa's Muslims. They also constitute the largest minority group in the region: approximately 300,000 people, living in Kenya and Tanzania. At one time, Uganda also had a large Asian community, which controlled much of the country's commercial life. In August 1972, however, 18 months after seizing power, the wildly impulsive President Amin took a huge step towards his nation's economic ruin by ordering all the 30,000 Asians without Ugandan nationality to leave within three months.

Historically, Europeans have had a far greater influence on East Africa than either Asians or Arabs. Today, however, they make up the smallest minority group in the region; they number about 40,000 in Kenya, 15,000 in Tanzania and no more than 4,000 in Uganda, most of them British. Less than 10 per cent are East African citizens; and, unlike the Asians and the Arabs, most of them tend to spend only a part of their working lives in East Africa, the majority regularly returning to their home countries on leave and ultimately retiring there.

One of the enduring testimonials of the European presence is Christianity, brought to the area by English and German missionaries. More than 70 per cent of Kenya's population is now Christian, while the figures for Uganda and Tanzania are about 60 per cent and 40 per cent respectively. Following the missionaries were the colonial administrators, planters and businessmen. Again, they were relatively few in number, but their influence was extraordinary. By developing railways and by imposing labour migration to plantations, farms and towns, they drastically altered the human geography of the region for all time.

Despite the existence of the Swahili coastal towns, the overwhelming majority of East Africans had no experience of urban living until well into the 20th century. Beyond the maritime strip, almost all the inhabitants of the region were either farmers or pastoralists. They were divided into a multitude of small, separate communities, and their traditional self-sufficient and self-governing ways meant that there was simply no need for them to establish any permanent trading or administrative centres.

The farmers, who had no equipment more sophisticated than iron-shod hoes, lived more or less permanently in villages, working small plots of land to provide enough food for their family's basic needs and bartering any surplus. The pastoralists, by contrast, were semi-nomadic herders who practised transhumance—that is, regularly moving their cattle from dry-season camps to wet-season camps, and sometimes covering enormous distances.

For both farmers and pastoralists alike, the basis of the social order was the family. From this simple foundation a staggering range of lifestyles

Zanzibaris take an evening dip as the sinking sun gilds waterside buildings on their island's west coast. United with Tanganyika in 1964 to form Tanzania, Zanzibar is linked to the mainland 35 kilometres away by a daily flight from Dar es Salaam.

1

evolved. But all social groups, from such highly organized societies as the monarchical Ganda to the present-day clans of wandering herdsmen, had two things in common: a reverence for their elders and a strict code of behaviour amongst close kin. The extended family of children, parents, aunts, uncles, cousins and grandparents remained all-important. Relatives were expected to help one another in times of need, and everyone was expected to honour and respect the aged.

A social system based on such recognized obligations worked because most peoples of the region had learnt to live without striving for wealth beyond their basic needs. Production surpluses for trading were kept to a modest level, and it was generally accepted that the effective sharing of resources was indispensable to the welfare of each individual community. Thus, a rough and ready egalitarianism became the basis of social peace and security. An unwritten moral code specified that no individual should attempt to get a notably larger share of the available food or materials than his neighbours, because the resultant inequality might dangerously disturb the balance of community life.

The essence of this centuries-old social order has been succinctly expressed by Professor Colin Turnbull, one of the world's foremost authorities on African life. "In traditional African societies," he wrote, "people relate to each other as human beings, not as mere cogs in some impersonal social machine. They obtain social security not through the manipulation of wealth in the form of cash, but through the creation of a network of effective, interlocking human relations. In such a society, economic wealth becomes re-latively insignificant, and perhaps thereby man becomes all the richer."

However, these traditional human values are now being challenged. Ever since British and German colonists introduced Western economic ideas to East Africa in the late 19th century, a new spirit of competition and profit-seeking has been abroad in the land, in conflict with the older, co-operative ways of the inhabitants. Such individualism has flourished all the more strongly with the growth of cities and towns where Africans, working away from home, have had the novel experience of earning a salary for providing services to people with whom they have no bond of kinship.

The most spectacular urban development has been in Nairobi, the capital of Kenya. The city originated at the beginning of the 20th century as a workshop on the half-constructed railway being built by the British to link Mombasa with the north-east shore of Lake Victoria in Uganda. It was so wild and remote in those days that the first six people to be buried in its cemetery were victims of man-eating lions. Since those days, however, Nairobi has grown from a one-shop, one-hotel only encampment into the largest city between Cairo and Johannesburg—a metropolis of more than 800,000 inhabitants, complete with skyscrapers, dual carriageways, night-clubs, cinemas, theatres, museums, art galleries and a university. It is more than twice the size of Mombasa, which it succeeded as capital of British East Africa in 1905, and almost six times the size of Kenya's third largest town, Kisumu, on Lake Victoria.

As a centre for European farmer-settlers, Nairobi had much to recommend it. Lying 1,800 metres up on the plateau to the east of the Great Rift Valley, its advantages include a relatively salubrious climate and a good water supply (in the Masai tongue *Nairobi* means "the place of cold water"). It is not so ideally sited for its present-day role as the modern capital since it lies far from the country's most populous areas on the margins of Lake Victoria. Nevertheless, its position as the political and commercial heart of Kenya is secure, especially since the establishment in the late 1940s of an industrial area to the east of the city. This centre now encompasses a range of light-to-medium industrial activities that make Kenya East Africa's most industrialized country.

Dar es Salaam, the major city of Tanzania, is a little older than Nairobi, having been established in 1866 by the Sultan of Zanzibar. He also gave it its name, meaning "Haven of Peace". Its deep harbour made it an ideal port and trading centre, and gradually it became the principal anchorage on the mainland, taking over from Bagamoyo 65 kilometres to the north, the ancient terminus of the ivory caravan routes. But, yet again, European colonists—in this instance the Germans, who had ousted the Arabs in 1887—were chiefly responsible for the modern development of the city.

With a population of more than 700,000, Dar es Salaam is almost as large as Nairobi, yet it is markedly less metropolitan in atmosphere. Much of the city centre consists of narrow, winding, tree-lined avenues and its buildings are only two or three storeys high. Its harbour, fronted with buildings of the German era, provides perhaps the most attractive setting of all East African cities. But again, like Nairobi, the city is not especially well

Primary schoolchildren board a bus
that will take them on a field trip to
Nairobi National Park, an 18-hectare
game reserve within the city limits.
Kenya has over 1,000 wildlife clubs
that organize outings to make children
more aware of their natural heritage.

placed to serve as the hub of its country. Therefore, in 1973, the Tanzanian government decided to transfer the capital 470 kilometres inland, to Dodoma. The move was designed to shift the nation's focus from the coast to the countryside, in order to reduce the colonial emphasis on exports and to stress the rural basis of the economy. But owing to lack of funds this new orientation has still not occurred. Lying on the great barren plateau at the centre of the country, Dodoma has a population of barely 50,000, and most of the government offices have remained in Dar es Salaam.

Kampala, the capital of Uganda, is the only East African city with some claim to purely African roots since it was built close to the court of the ancient rulers (Kabakas) of Buganda. The Bugandan court comprised about 500 buildings, and was the centre of a population of about 20,000 when European explorers first visited the kingdom in the 1860s. The British built a fort on a nearby hill, named Kampala after the impala antelope. But they chose to establish the capital of their Uganda protectorate at Entebbe, 30 kilometres away at the end of a peninsula jutting into Lake Victoria. While Entebbe remained strictly a preserve of British officialdom, Kampala established itself as the centre of Uganda's commercial, social, political and religious life—and thus the logical choice of capital city after the gaining of national independence.

The layout of the city reveals the influences that have helped to shape the nation of Uganda. It now covers a cluster of hills, each dominated by some kind of centre of national or historical importance. Mengo Hill, once the site of the Kabaka's Palace, now contains a military barracks. Kampala Hill is crowned with the remains of the original British fort; and the nearby Nakesero Hill—the new focus of power—is the site of a modern barracks, government offices, parliament buildings, the High Court, the national radio station, as well as the city's main shopping and entertainment areas.

About half a million people occupy the undulating streets of this capital, which dominates Uganda's urban life to an astonishing degree. By comparison, a mere 45,000 people live in Jinja,

the country's second largest town and main industrial centre, which lies 80 kilometres to the east, close by the Owen Falls Dam and power station.

All of East Africa's cities clearly manifest European influence in their central architecture and their layout. Within the cities, however, urban life differs quite radically from any Western model. Many of their inhabitants are desperately poor, even though the poverty may not be readily apparent to the casual visitor; slum areas are invariably located on the outskirts of town, where few tourists or visiting business people are likely to venture. There, the bulk of the urban population live in crowded shanty towns with only the most basic amenities.

The inhabitants of these slums are mostly refugees from rural distress, drawn to the cities in search of wealth and opportunity. In fact, the unending influx of country folk only heightens

the problem of urban unemployment and food shortages while also reducing the manpower for agricultural development. From time to time, governments have attempted to combat the problem by evicting squatters, but with little success. In Nairobi, for example, the squatters are so well organized that they can dismantle their shanties at daybreak and re-erect them at nightfall.

Significantly, the city populations are extremely youthful: more than 25 per cent of the inhabitants are under 10 years of age, while fewer than 10 per cent are over 50. People over 65 years old constitute only 1.5 per cent of the population in Dar es Salaam and 1.1 per cent in Nairobi. High birth rates go some way to explaining such youth-orientated population profiles, as does the large number of students in the cities. Life expectancy, too, for the three countries averages just 52.3 years. But the main reason for the paucity of old people is that most urban dwellers choose to return to their homes and kin in the rural areas when they are too old to work in the towns. Family ties are still the chief form of security for the majority of East Africans, and the land remains essentially the place where they have their roots.

In time, of course, the traditional social structure of East Africa will be comprehensively changed as, for better or worse, more and more people are drawn into the cash economy. Already, the countryside—the repository of traditional values—is in flux since the introduction of new farming techniques involving fertilizers, improved crop strains and irrigation schemes, and the setting up of marketing co-operatives to reduce middleman costs for farmers. Such innovations are effectively en-

In a fertile rural area of eastern Uganda, banana trees crowd round a family homestead built of wooden poles and reeds rendered with mud and cow dung. Unusually, the building boasts two storeys, with a ladder inside giving access to the upper floor.

couraging smallholders to raise production far beyond their basic needs. At the same time, in many far-flung areas, schools and dispensaries are being built to encourage pastoralists to settle in permanent villages.

To be sure, the iron hoe is still the principal agricultural implement of the masses; and the majority of people still build their own houses with dried mud, and with wood, thatch and other materials gathered from the bush surrounding them. But although many of the communities are located enormous distances from the main roads and rail-way arteries, there are now very few where the modern world has not visibly penetrated to some degree, if only in the shape of such cash-bought possessions as bicycles, machine-made clothes and radios.

Throughout the region, the rate of social change has been astonishing when one considers that only a century ago the peoples of East Africa, save those along the narrow coastal strip, had no knowledge of either literacy or machinery, and had not even the use of equipment fitted with wheels. Politically, too, there have been far-reaching developments as tribal peoples have struggled to come to terms with the modern nation-state. For better or for worse, old African ways have been transformed by an onrush of events set in motion by the arrival of the first Europeans almost five hundred years ago. That epic confrontation of vastly differing cultures, and the subsequent experience of colonization and the struggle for liberation that ensued, are the essential scene-setters for any understanding of the present-day realities of the lands where the earliest known humans used to live.

BIG GAME IN A BIG COUNTRY

Formed on a prodigious scale, East Africa's diverse landscapes and dramatic vistas provide fittingly spectacular settings for the world's greatest concentrations of big game animals. Vast herds of herbivores and their predators roam free in sparsely peopled terrains embracing snow-capped mountains, volcanic craters, soda flats and seemingly limitless stretches of woodland and savannah. Visitors can witness a pristine splendour that has changed little since our hominoid ancestors emerged here more than three million years ago.

This unique natural heritage is so crucial to tourism that all three East African countries have increased the size and number of their game reserves since gaining independence. Kenya alone has nearly 40 conservation areas, ranging in size from enclaves of a few hundred hectares to self-contained animal kingdoms such as the Tsavo National Park, where lions rule a wilderness covering 20,720 square kilometres. The country even boasts a national wildlife park within the city limits of its capital, Nairobi.

In Tanzania, national parks, game reserves and forest reserves take up nearly one quarter of the land—a higher proportion than in any other country in the world. Largely spread over open woodland, the preserves cannot match the scenic variety found in Kenya or in Uganda, which was once called "The Pearl of Africa" because of its glorious landscapes and lush, fertile zones. But Tanzania, too, has views of great splendour, most especially in its far north, which includes Africa's highest mountain, Kilimanjaro; one of the world's largest craters, Ngorongoro; and numerous small volcanoes and conical cinder mounds that conjure up visions of the moon.

With the snow-capped mass of
Tanzania's Mount Kilimanjaro forming
a suitably majestic backdrop, a lion
sprawls at regal ease in Kenya's
Amboseli National Park. Designated a
park in 1973, Amboseli still has some
Masai herdsmen, who have co-existed
with the wild game for centuries.

A pair of cheetahs pad across the soda
flats of Ngurdoto Crater in Tanzania's
Arusha National Park. Within its 117
square kilometres, the park includes
open terrain that is ideal hunting
ground for cheetahs—the fastest of
land animals, with an explosive sprint
approaching 100 kilometres per hour.

A flock of flamingoes—one of the most numerous species in East Africa—fills a soda lake at the centre of Tanzania's Ngorongoro Crater. The birds feed on algae and shrimps—the only creatures that are able to survive in such lakes, which are saturated with chemicals leached from volcanic ash.

A mixed herd of grazing animals congregates by a water hole in Kenya's arid Tsavo National Park. In the foreground, marabou storks wait impassively.

The largest of their genus, these carrion-eaters are attracted to watering places because herbivores are most vulnerable to predators when drinking.

Buffaloes graze on the wet-season greenery of Serengeti National Park, inhabited by more than 30 species of large herbivores, including some two million wildebeest. Covering 14,700 square kilometres, the park boasts one of the most complex and least disturbed ecosystems on earth.

Members of a hyena clan briefly shift their attention from wildebeest in the Ngorongoro Crater. Long reviled as cowardly scavengers, hyenas are actually formidable predators, capable of relentlessly chasing their prey at 60 kilometres per hour and biting through a wildebeest's thighbone with ease.

Cattle egrets fly over a herd of elephants in Uganda's Kabalega National Park. At one time the park was a sanctuary for as many as 8,000 elephants and a

population of rare white rhinoceros, but during Uganda's civil wars many of the animals were killed by poachers or lawless bands of soldiers.

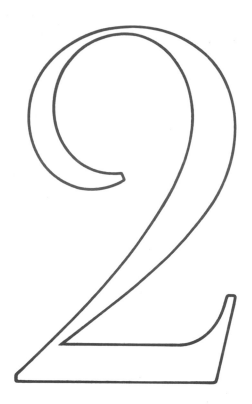

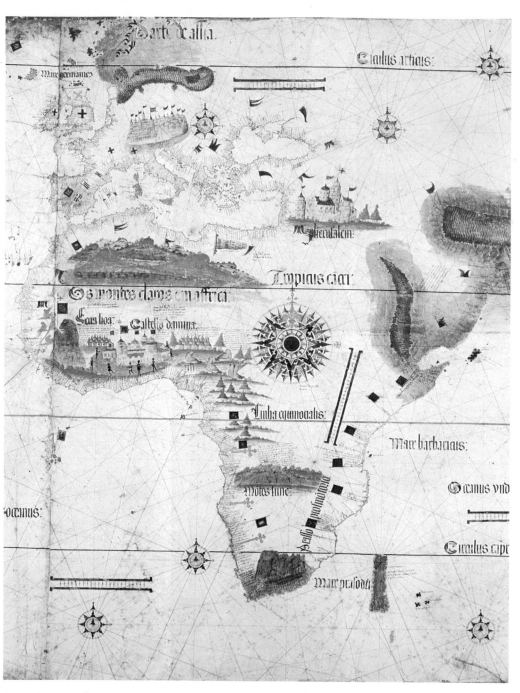

A detail from a Portuguese world map of 1502 shows that by that date European explorers had already accurately charted the outline of Africa. Seeking tribute and plunder, the newcomers were to make a disastrous impact on the trading ports of the eastern coast.

THE EUROPEAN INVASION

On Saturday, July 8, 1497, four ships and 170 men under the command of Captain Major Vasco da Gama set sail from Lisbon on the greatest maritime venture in Portugal's long seafaring history: a 40,000-kilometre round-trip voyage to establish an ocean-route to India. In November, they rounded the Cape of Good Hope. On Christmas Day they gave the name Natal to a stretch of gently sloping uplands on their port-side. Then, early in the New Year, they became the first Europeans to reach East Africa. What they found filled them with wonder and relief.

They came prepared to encounter a wilderness inhabited by half-naked, hostile barbarians. Instead, the land seemed a veritable El Dorado—a region fringed by prosperous independent city-states, with whitewashed houses veiled in flowering vines, and gleaming mosques and slender minarets that pierced the coastal skyline. They met sultans who ruled in regal splendour, and Arabs dressed in fine linen robes and silk gold-embroidered turbans who traded cotton, ivory, timber and gold for Chinese porcelain, Persian rubies and Indian spices.

Earlier, in the extreme south of Africa, the Portuguese adventurers had met scantily dressed natives who received with glee their barter of glass beads, bracelets, bells and rings. Now, in the east, they found such trinkets were relatively worthless. At the gold-rich city of Mozambique, the expedition's diarist recorded that the local sultan "treated all we gave him with contempt and asked for scarlet cloth, of which we had none". Some 1,300 kilometres north, they came to Mombasa, the area's most populous city, where 10,000 citizens lived on a steamy, palm-fringed island hard by the mainland. Again, they failed to impress with their offerings. Indeed, they met with positive hostility after proclaiming their Christianity to a people busy celebrating the end of fasting during the Muslim month of Ramadan.

A further 80 kilometres north, on Easter Sunday, the Portuguese arrived at Malindi, a smaller city on the coast of present-day Kenya. Here, at last, they received a friendly welcome from a sultan who saw them as a possible ally to oppose his great rival in Mombasa. The sultan provided gifts of cloves, ginger, nutmeg and pepper— and, most valuable of all, a navigator for their voyage ahead. As a result, the Portuguese triumphed in their mission to find a sea route to India. The perilous two-year expedition cost them almost a third of their men. The cost to East Africa, however, was infinitely greater. Indeed, the arrival of Europeans proved to be the most fateful event in the region's turbulent history.

Today, in the Western world, the popular history of East Africa is seen as an epic dominated by the heroic deeds of an extraordinary array of daredevil explorers, missionaries and adventurers. But viewed through African eyes that history is largely a catalogue of tragedies set in motion by European intruders who purported, as Christians, to be performing a civilizing mission. The Portuguese set the pattern at the dawn of the 16th century. Initially, they hoped to make treaties with the Arabs and Swahili who had established themselves in city-states along a 3,000-kilometre stretch of coastal plain and on adjoining islands. When they failed to achieve a profitable trade by peaceful means, they resorted to force.

On his second voyage, in 1502, Vasco da Gama landed at the city of Kilwa in present-day Tanzania and compelled the sultan to submit and pay tribute to the King of Portugal. The next year, another Portuguese expedition forced Zanzibar to do the same. Then, in 1505, the nobleman Francisco de Almeida, given the grand title of Viceroy of India, set sail with a cannon-laden fleet. En route to the Indies, he ruthlessly sacked and destroyed East African coastal cities that had refused to meet his nation's demands.

Off Kilwa, a Portuguese historian recorded: "From our ships, the fine houses, terraces and minarets, with the palm trees in the orchards, made the city look so beautiful that our men were eager to land and overcome the pride of this barbarian." Dom Francisco landed with 500 men and, without much resistance (bows and arrows were no match for Portuguese steel), pillaged the town and appointed a new sultan. Leaving behind a small garrison, he sailed on to Mombasa and reduced that large, stylish town to ruins littered with more than 1,500 dead.

By 1510, whether by threat, conquest or treaty, all the East African city-states had been brought under Portuguese hegemony. But the European invaders did not colonize or develop the coast. They merely built strong forts to protect their trade, which was principally in ivory and ambergris. They had little interest in the region's economic development, or in spreading Christianity. And, overall, their influence was dismal. Known to the Swahili as *afriti*, or devils, the Portuguese disrupted Indian Ocean trade, crippled local merchants, and in the process failed to make substantial profits for themselves.

Gradually, most of the great city-states fell into ruin and decay. In a desperate bid to oust the Portuguese, the Swahili turned for military assistance to the state of Oman in southern Arabia. The alliance only served to make them subject to even more demanding masters. By the 1820s, the Omani Arabs, aided by mercenary troops from Baluchistan (now a province of Pakistan), had seized command of most of the Swahili seaboard from northern Kenya to southern Tanzania. With them they brought the greatest misery inflicted upon East Africa's peoples—a steadily mounting slave trade which continued on an appalling scale far into the 19th century.

In 1840, the all-powerful Sultan of Oman, Sayyid Said, transferred his capital from scorching Muscat to the balmier climate of Zanzibar. By then, his slave-raiders were penetrating deep into the interior along old trails opened up by Swahili traders. According to a British estimate, slave sales in Zanzibar had already risen to between 40,000 and 45,000 victims a year, and these numbers rapidly rose higher still. Some slaves from the interior were put to work on Sultan Said's clove plantations in Zanzibar, but many more were shipped to the Red Sea and the Persian Gulf, or sold to European buyers for transport to the Americas.

By this time the British had pulled out of the slave trade, having banned it from all their ships in 1807. But the French had begun importing mainland African captives for use as plantation slaves on Indian Ocean islands such as Mauritius, and the Portuguese were transporting large numbers to Brazil. In the mid-19th century, probably as many as 100,000 East Africans were sold into overseas enslavement every year. This infamous traffic did not finally end until the 1880s, and it was to be many years before the region's vic-timized peoples could fully recover from the ruin and depopulation.

Meanwhile, an event of considerable significance had occurred, though its importance was little realized then. In 1823, a British naval captain, one William Fitzwilliam Wentworth Owen, was commanding two ships charting the East African coast for the Admiralty at a time when the port of Mombasa was being threatened by an Omani fleet. As a devout Christian, Owen took it upon himself to lecture Sultan Said on the evils of the slave trade, and subsequently he agreed to give official British protection to the people of Mombasa on condition that they abolished slavery forthwith.

Thus, for the first time the Union Jack was hoisted in East Africa. The captain's move was entirely contrary to the foreign policy of the British government, which had no wish to make an enemy of Oman or take on a costly commitment in a remote coastal town of no obvious commercial or strategic importance. Owen, with a sense of duty more religious than naval, had acted entirely alone. In a dispatch to the Admiralty, he declared that he had been influenced by no personal motive whatever. "It is to me as clear as the sun that God has prepared the dominion of East Africa for the only nation on earth that has public virtue enough to govern it for its own benefit and for the only people who take the revealed word for their moral law."

In due course, the British government cancelled Owen's establishment of a "British protectorate of Mombasa" and the local slave trade flourished anew. But the period of European empire in East Africa was now on its way. With the British navy supreme in eastern seas, Zanzibar itself came under

A late-19th-century silver and gold comb—one of six designed for the harem of a sultan of Zanzibar— exemplifies the richness and elegance of Swahili craftsmanship. The Swahili civilization evolved on the coast from a blending of African and Arab cultures.

British suzerainty in the 1850s, partly as a means of halting the Zanzibari slave trade. Soon after, Britain and Germany began vying for power in mainland East Africa, and in 1890 they agreed to formally recognize their respective spheres of influence. Zanzibar became a British protectorate, effectively a colony, and the future colonies of British East Africa—later Kenya—and German East Africa—the future Tanganyika—began to take shape.

For 350 years after the East African coast was first visited by Europeans, the lands that backed it remained *terra incognita*. Not until the late 1840s did explorers finally pluck up courage to venture more than a few kilometres into the interior. Two Mombasa-based German missionaries, Johann Rebmann and Johann Ludwig Krapf, led the way by organizing expeditions aimed at converting Africans to Christianity. The former, in 1846, was the first European to set eyes on snow-capped Mount Kilimanjaro; the latter, three years later, discovered Mount Kenya. But their pioneering exploits, achieved in the face of extreme danger and personal hardship, earned them only derision. In faraway London, members of the Royal Geographical Society branded them liars or hoaxers. Snow, they agreed, was a physical impossibility so close to the equator.

There was less scepticism in 1855 when another German missionary, James Erhardt, produced a map of the East African interior based on third-hand information given to his compatriots by Arab and Swahili ivory traders. It became known as the "slug map" because it depicted a slug-shaped inland sea called Uniamuesi, beyond which, Erhardt believed, lay

Africa's legendary Mountains of the Moon—named by the Egyptian-born mathematician-geographer Ptolemy in his famous *Geographia*, dated about 150 A.D. According to Ptolemy, this great range fed two lakes which were the twin sources of the Nile.

In Europe, the "slug map" aroused fresh interest in the source of Africa's greatest river. The origin of the Blue Nile—the river's northern arm, which springs 1,800 metres up in the highlands of Ethiopia—had been settled in 1770 by James Bruce, a Scottish aristocrat-explorer. But another, much larger arm—the White Nile—was known to rise far to the south, presumably somewhere in the East African hinterland. Spurred by the appearance of the "slug map", the Royal Geographical Society raised enough funds for an expedition to solve the mystery that had puzzled and intrigued men since

the days of the pharaohs. Its chosen leader was Richard Burton, a 35-year-old lieutenant in the East India Company's Bombay Light Infantry.

Burton, a multilingual adventurer of towering intellect and insatiable curiosity, is now best remembered as the translator of great classics of Eastern erotica: the *Kama Sutra*, the *Perfumed Garden* and *Arabian Nights*. In 1856, however, his fame rested largely on his exploits in Somalia. Two years earlier he had become the first white man to enter the forbidden city of Harar, at that time the religious capital of Muslim Somalia; then, miraculously, he had survived an attack on his 42-man expedition by 350 tribesmen hurling javelins and daggers. In this assault, one British officer was fatally speared; another, Lieut. John Hanning Speke, received 11 wounds. Burton himself escaped with "a javelin through both

EXPLORERS OF THE DARK CONTINENT

Between 1857 and 1877, a succession of explorers sought to solve one of the last great mysteries of geography: the whereabouts of the source of the Nile. The way was pioneered by Richard Burton and John Speke, the first Europeans to see Lake Tanganyika *(map, far right)*. The latter went on to reach Lake Victoria, which he proclaimed as the source. That claim—challenged by Burton—was still unconfirmed after a second expedition by Speke and fellow-officer James Grant, and after Samuel Baker had identified Lake Albert as a possible headwater.

To settle the controversy, Dr. David Livingstone set out in 1867 on his last journey—one so prolonged that H.M. Stanley of the *New York Herald* was sent out to locate him. The two met at Ujiji in 1871. Two years later Livingstone died while still in search of the source.

It was left to Stanley, on his 1874–77 expedition, to solve the puzzle by circumnavigating Lake Victoria and establishing it once and for all as the fountainhead of the world's longest river. Thereafter, explorers found new challenges—most notably in the region of present-day Kenya, which was largely opened up by the Scottish geologist Joseph Thomson.

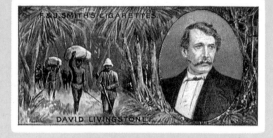

John H. Speke (1827–64) was one of three great East African explorers featured in a 1911 series of cigarette cards *(left and below)*. He located and named Lake Victoria, and made the first European contact with the kingdom of Buganda. Aged 37, he died in a shooting accident before his claim to have found the source of the Nile was substantiated.

David Livingstone (1813–73) left school at 10 to work in a cotton mill. Qualifying as a missionary-doctor in 1840, he at once embarked for Africa, where he walked across the entire continent, traced the Zambezi river and discovered Victoria Falls and Lakes Ngami and Malawi. He died in Africa, and was buried in Westminster Abbey in 1874.

Henry Morton Stanley (1841–1904) was born in Wales, the illegitimate son of a farmer. Reaching New Orleans as a cabin boy, he became a roving reporter for the *New York Herald*. In 1869 he was sent to find Livingstone. Subsequently, he explored East Africa's lakes and the Congo. Knighted in 1899, he ended his career as a British M.P.

cheeks, carrying away four teeth and transfixing the palate". Yet this grievous injury did not discourage him from seizing the opportunity to return to Africa and seek the source of the Nile. And Speke was no less eager to accompany him.

In June 1857, Burton and Speke set out from Zanzibar with 130 porters and 30 donkeys laden with *hongo*—trade goods and trinkets to be given away in exchange for safe passage. It was a pioneering journey that was to take them across the centre of what is now mainland Tanzania. Eight months later, after enduring terrible hardships, they came upon a vast body of water never before seen by Europeans—Lake Tanganyika. They suspected, wrongly, that this was the main source of the Nile. However, on the return march, when Burton was racked with sickness, Speke independently struck northwards and located another great lake. He named it after Queen Victoria, and concluded, intuitively, that this was the true "fountainhead of the Nile". Burton disagreed. Nevertheless, Speke reaped enormous kudos from his discovery. Returning to England ahead of Burton, he lectured to the Royal Geographical Society on his findings, and subsequently he was

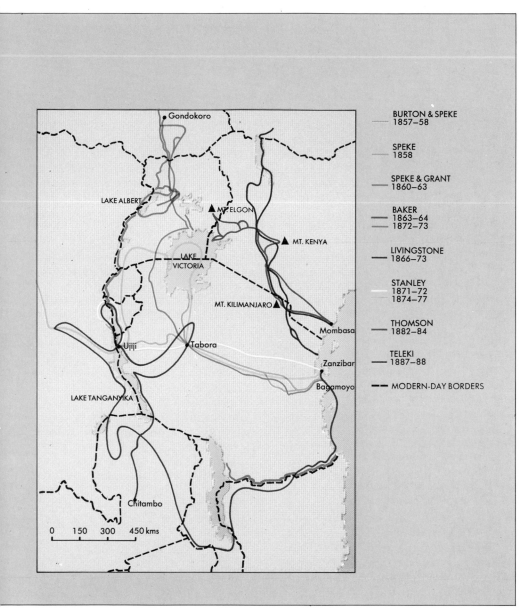

BURTON & SPEKE
1857-58

SPEKE
1858

SPEKE & GRANT
1860-63

BAKER
1863-64
1872-73

LIVINGSTONE
1866-73

STANLEY
1871-72
1874-77

THOMSON
1882-84

TELEKI
1887-88

--- MODERN-DAY BORDERS

lakeside territory ruled over by Mutesa, the most powerful of the three kings who then reigned in the territory now occupied by southern Uganda. Its Ganda residents, like all the peoples of Uganda, were relatively sophisticated. They boasted advanced crafts and techniques, as shown in their construction of 20-metre-long war canoes and 15-metre-high conical buildings; and they also had a hierarchical system of government whereby their kabaka was advised by a group of counsellors with clearly defined positions, ranging from commander-in-chief to chief brewer. But they did not have the wheel or the plough, and they were ruled by a fierce despot. On his succession, Mutesa had burnt his 60 brothers alive—one of several grisly Ugandan traditions used to forestall intra-dynastic rebellion. Thereafter, he commonly ordered executions for his own amusement. Children who did not attend his words were liable to have their ears lopped off.

Speke and his men were detained in Buganda, virtually as prisoners, for almost six months. Finally, the Kabaka permitted them to leave and, in July 1862, Speke located the point where Lake Victoria emptied into the Nile, 80 kilometres east of present-day Kampala. The following year, on reaching Cairo, he cabled the Royal Geographical Society: "The Nile is settled." But it was not. He had failed to circumnavigate Lake Victoria to establish that no rivers entered it. Therefore, his claim remained open to challenge—especially by Burton who favoured Lake Tanganyika as the fountainhead.

In September 1864, Burton and Speke were due to debate publicly their fiercely opposed views. But on the eve of the debate, Speke—a hunter of supreme expertise—was killed by his

given command of a second expedition dispatched to explore Lake Victoria more thoroughly.

The follow-up expedition—an epic three-year journey from Zanzibar to Lake Victoria, then down the length of the 6,648-kilometre River Nile—left the east coast near Bagamoyo on October 2, 1860. After nearly 14 months the party had covered only about 1,000 kilometres to reach Karagwe, a kingdom on the edge of Uganda between the western shores of Lake Victoria and the Virunga Mountains. There the explorers were entertained by Ruwanika, a most hospitable, inquisitive king, whose numerous milk-fattened wives were so obese that they were unable to stand upright and could move only on their hands and knees.

To reach Lake Victoria, Speke then had to enter Buganda, a neighbouring

2

own hand while shooting birds in the English countryside. He was 37 years old. Officially an accidental death, some acquaintances concluded that Speke had committed suicide rather than have his none-too-scientific arguments demolished. Burton wrote to a friend: "The charitable say that he shot himself, the uncharitable that I shot him." The irony was that Speke had been more or less right all along.

But this was still unproven in 1864. In Britain, the mystery of the Nile's source had become a national obsession, and by popular consent one man was best equipped to settle the issue: Dr. David Livingstone, the Scottish missionary who had been the first European to cross the Kalahari Desert, who had traversed the African continent from the Atlantic to the Indian Ocean, and who numbered among his discoveries the Zambezi river, Lakes Ngami and Malawi, and "the smoke that thunders", the mighty Victoria Falls. At the invitation of the Royal Geographical Society, this greatest of all African explorers agreed to lead an expedition on condition that missionary work should take precedence over geographical discovery. His personal theory was that both Burton and Speke were wrong; he suspected that the Nile might rise much further south, possibly flowing through one of their great lakes on its way to the north.

It was on this expedition that Livingstone had his historic encounter with Henry Morton Stanley, the young *New York Herald* journalist sent out to search for the explorer after three years had passed without news of his whereabouts. They met in November 1871, at Ujiji, a great Arab slaving station on the eastern shore of Lake Tanganyika, and together went on to explore the

northerly end of the lake. Livingstone, by now a self-styled "rackle of bones", later set out alone to continue his search for the source of the Nile. It was his final journey. On May 1, 1873, in a remote village in what is now Zambia, his servants found him dead, slumped on his knees as if in prayer.

Devotedly, the African servants cut out their master's heart and viscera, and buried them under a tree. His body was dried in the sun for a fortnight, then wrapped in calico and fitted into a cylinder of bark which, in turn, was wrapped in sailcloth and lashed to poles. Subsequently, they made a nine-month, 2,500-kilometre trek to carry his embalmed body back to the coast. More than 700 freed slaves came to pay their respects at Bagamoyo, before the corpse was shipped to Zanzibar, then England, where Livingstone was laid to rest in Westminster Abbey. His heart, appropriately, was left where it belonged—in Africa.

What set Livingstone apart from other African explorers was not just the scale of his achievements, but also the sympathy and understanding—paternalistic but sincere—he conveyed to the African peoples, whose languages he assiduously learnt and whose customs he meticulously noted. His greatest humanitarian work was in waging war on the slave trade which, though banned throughout most of West Africa, continued to flourish in East Africa until the 1880s.

Henry Stanley, in contrast, felt no deep attachment to Africa and its people. "I detest the land most heartily," he wrote. "I am seldom well enough for a day or two when steeped in quinine." Yet he so idolized Livingstone that he resolved to complete the great man's mission as an explorer.

Indeed, on an expedition lasting three years, 1874 to 1877, he accomplished much more. He settled once and for all the mystery of the White Nile, tracing its headwater, the Kagera river, from Lake Victoria to a source 2,500 metres up in the mountains of southern Burundi, about 50 kilometres short of Lake Tanganyika. Therefore Speke's claims were at least partly vindicated, and Burton was proved wrong. Stanley then went on to discover Lake Edward, due west of Lake Victoria.

During his travels, Stanley spent some time at the court of the Kabaka of Buganda. He came away with impressions far more favourable than those of Speke. He reported on the "pleasing civility" of a splendid and well-ordered kingdom, and noted Mutesa's interest in Christianity. Moreover, he persuaded the Kabaka to allow a permanent mission to be established in Buganda. As a result, in 1876, both Anglican and Catholic missionaries arrived, and subsequently vied for influence with rival clans and peoples of the region. The Anglican mission marked the beginning of a permanent British presence in the East African interior, and indirectly it laid the foundation of the future British protectorate in Uganda.

The epic journeys of Stanley, and of Burton, Speke and Livingstone before him, criss-crossed the territory of what is now Tanzania and southern Uganda, but left the northern regions of East Africa still uncharted. Kenya especially had been neglected by explorers—to such a degree that up to the early 1880s no Westerner had verified the much-derided reports of snow-capped mountains made by Rebmann and Krapf over 30 years before. In part, this was due to the attention focused on the quest for the source of the Nile. But a

On board the store ship, H.M.S. *London*, newly freed slaves pose for a picture publicizing the work of Britain's anti-slavery patrols off the East African coast. The slave traffic was banned in 1873, but not effectively halted until the turn of the century.

significant factor was the presence of a tribal community of exceptionally fearsome reputation: the Masai.

The Masai are a nomadic, cattle-herding people whose homelands, well suited to pastoral life, bestraddle the present-day Kenya-Tanzania border. In the 19th century, they numbered perhaps 50,000, and their warriors, renowned for their fighting prowess, were indeed frightening to behold: tall, lean, red-ochred and usually adorned with a lion-mane headdress. As a well-disciplined, guerrilla-style force, they not only jealously guarded their own territory, but, unlike most tribal groups, roamed far and wide to raid other communities. Quite simply, the Masai warrior lived for battle.

One of the first Europeans to face up to the challenge of Masailand was Joseph Thomson, a young Scottish geologist so fascinated by Africa that he had unsuccessfully volunteered to join Stanley's search for Livingstone when he was only 11 years old. Fourteen years later, in 1883, he was leader of his own expedition, appointed by the Royal Geographical Society to explore the region of Mount Kenya and to ascertain if there was a practical direct route from the coast to the potentially profitable kingdoms of Uganda. With him were 113 porters recruited with great difficulty in Zanzibar. "The very idea of going to the dreaded Masai country," he wrote, "was sufficient to take their breath away."

On the expedition, Thomson walked almost 5,000 kilometres in 14 months, and survived threatening encounters not only with the Masai but also with the Kikuyu and Luo people (then called Kavirondo). His greatest aid to survival was his own inventiveness. On

THE LUNATIC LINE

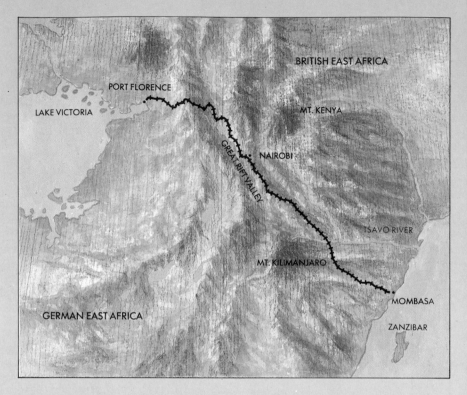

Obsessed by the need to protect the headwaters of the Nile, in 1896 the British began to build a railway for transporting troops from the coast at Mombasa to the north-east shore of Lake Victoria in Uganda. The project involved laying nearly 1,000 kilometres of track over seemingly impossible terrain; in Parliament its critics dubbed it the "lunatic line".

It was a nightmarish enterprise from the start. The debilitating coastal climate played havoc with schedules, as did the crossing of scorched, waterless desert followed by hill country and tangled thornbush infested with tsetse flies. Shortage of African labour necessitated the importing of 32,000 Indian workers. Then man-eating lions and enraged rhinos terrorized construction teams. By May 1899, they had traversed 500 kilometres to establish a headquarters station at Nairobi. But ahead lay the sternest challenge: the Great Rift Valley, a chasm 800 metres deep in places.

It took another year and a half to cross that awesome gap and descend the final 150 kilometres to the shore of Lake Victoria. The first train steamed into the Port Florence terminus a year behind schedule, in 1901, though temporary railworks were not replaced until 1903. By then the project's cost had reached £5.5 million. The price in human terms was 2,500 workers dead and 6,500 injured. But their sacrifice, like the original purpose of the line, was soon forgotten as settlers moved in along the railway's path.

Until viaducts bridged the steepest gradients, platforms bearing men and equipment were winched down into the Great Rift Valley.

Beyond Nairobi, an Indian plate-laying gang rests before tackling an incline on the way to the summit of the Rift Valley's eastern wall.

Rattling over hastily built trestle-bridges, trains carried the trade that helped finance 60 years of British rule in Kenya and Uganda.

2

one occasion, when faced with a band of hostile Masai, he stopped the warriors in their tracks by flourishing his false teeth and convincing them that he could remove a nose or an eye with equal facility. His other conjuring tricks included using a galvanic battery to challenge the courage of natives with a sharp but harmless shock, and bringing still liquid to life by dropping Eno's fruit salts into a glass of water. More important, for a while the Masai believed that he was expert in treating their livestock for rinderpest.

Largely by such ingenuity, Thomson survived to make the most spectacular exploration of northern East Africa. He skirted Mount Kilimanjaro and climbed the extinct volcano Longonot, 80 kilometres north of present-day Nairobi. He discovered nearby Lake Naivasha and crossed a range of mountains which he named after Lord Aberdare, a future president of the Royal Geographical Society. Then, by way of Mount Kenya, he reached the north-eastern shore of Lake Victoria. On the return journey, he discovered Mount Elgon. There, he was badly gored by a wounded buffalo; later, weakened by dysentery, he lay semiconscious for six weeks. Yet Thomson, quintessentially a romantic adventurer, continued to find Africa irresistible.

He made three more expeditions on which he drew up trade agreements with numerous East African chiefs. Finally, ruined health forced him to rest in England. He was still expressing a yearning for African adventure shortly before he died at the age of 37.

In Britain, Thomson had sustained popular interest in Africa by his exploits, and not least by his classic book *Through Masai Land*. In turn, this interest was boosted by an even more popular African adventure—the novel *King Solomon's Mines* by a young English lawyer, Henry Rider Haggard.

By the end of the 1880s, all the main geographical features of East Africa had been explored. A new chapter in the region's history was opening, as European interest focused less on adventure and more on the political and economic advantages to be gained by establishing footholds in such an inhospitable corner of the world. The "scramble for Africa" was about to begin—a gathering stampede so great that by the turn of the century seven European nations—Britain, France, Germany, Portugal, Belgium, Spain and Italy—had laid claim to vast territories on the African continent.

The man most responsible for the stampede into East Africa was Dr. Carl Peters, a German metaphysician who, in 1884, formed his own private organization, the Society for German Colonization, and subsequently negotiated a number of treaties of "Eternal Friendship" with chiefs in Tanzania. Initially, these treaties did not have the sanction of his government, but their effect was to transfer to Germany 4,000 square kilometres of land nominally ruled by the Sultan of Zanzibar.

By way of reply, Sir William Mackinnon, a Scottish businessman, negotiated a similar deal under which the Imperial British East African Company would administer the sultan's mainland territories in his name in return for virtual sovereignty over a 300-kilometre stretch of the Zanzibar coastal strip between the villages of Vanga and Kipini. He also engaged a remarkably enterprising young army officer, Frederick (later Lord) Lugard, to establish a major British presence in Uganda in face of direct opposition from the Germans, who were competing with Muslim Arabs and French and British missionaries for the ear of the Kabaka of Buganda.

The danger of a clash between the imperialist powers was now obvious. Prudently, they avoided confrontation by drawing up the 1890 Heligoland Treaty, whereby Germany recognized British claims to Uganda and the British acknowledged German presence south of a line starting south of Mombasa and drawn directly north-west to Lake Victoria, except for one small kink designed to make a birthday present of Mount Kilimanjaro to Queen Victoria's grandson, the Kaiser. In addition, the Treaty established Zanzibar as a British protectorate.

Britain, for her part, ceded to Germany the North Sea island of Heligoland, then regarded as a valuable naval base. Dr. Peters, the passionate patriot who had created for the Kaiser an empire twice the size of his own country, and who had toiled most courageously and ruthlessly to colonize Uganda, concluded in disgust that "two kingdoms in Africa had been bartered for a bathtub in the North Sea".

Until this time, the British government had been firmly opposed to any major commitment in East Africa beyond the coastal region, which provided useful naval stations along the southern sea lanes to British India. Inland, it was judged, the political and physical hazards were too formidable to merit commercial development. But now there was a new awareness—arguably much exaggerated—of the strategic importance of Uganda in relation to the Suez Canal, the vital short-cut to the East. Britain's long obsession with the quest for the source of the Nile had converted itself into a new axiom of imperial geopolitics: whichever nation controlled the headwaters of the White Nile would have the power to interfere with the flow of Egypt's life-blood. Neglecting the huge engineering problems that would have been involved in any attempt to dam the river, military strategists talked as though its water could be turned on and off like a tap, threatening the stability of Egypt. This fear increased after 1889, when a treaty negotiated with Abyssinia gave Italy territory along the banks of the Blue Nile.

As a result, the British government became receptive to an extravagant project championed by Sir William Mackinnon: the building of a railway from Mombasa to Lake Victoria. This, it was argued, would enable troops to be moved rapidly up-country if the Upper Nile were threatened. Further support was won by the argument that the opening up of the interior by rail would indirectly speed the demise of the slave trade. On the other hand, there was massive opposition on economic grounds, and the project was soon nicknamed the "lunatic line" by its opponents in Parliament. After all, it entailed laying nearly 1,000 kilometres of track over impossible terrain—across a sterile, waterless desert, over unmapped savannah and scrubland teeming with lions and buzzing with tsetse flies, through a volcanic region dissected by the yawning chasm of the Great Rift Valley, and over more than 150 kilometres of quagmire.

After years of impassioned political debate, the project was at last begun in December, 1895. A year later, the so-called Uganda Railway had advanced just 37 kilometres, partly because of an outbreak of malaria and dysentery, partly because of the absence of skilled labour among the local populace, few of whom were interested in working on the white man's iron road. If the railway was to succeed, more workers would have to be imported. And so they were brought in from India— eventually more than 30,000 of them, smiths, stonemasons, carpenters and unskilled labourers. In their wake came all sorts of diseases hitherto unknown in East Africa, plus a marked increase in syphilis. Initially, the Indian workers came on three-year contracts, but many were to stay on permanently to become merchants, shopkeepers and clerks.

In its second year, with the advantage of more skilled labour, the "lunatic line" advanced at four times its previous pace—as far as the Tsavo river, 210 kilometres from Mombasa. Tsavo is the local African word for slaughter—and appropriately so since here progress on the railway was seriously delayed by a pair of man-eating lions which terrorized the area for almost a year, killing 28 railway workers, as well as an uncounted number of African villagers. Usually, the lions attacked at night, dragging sleeping workmen from their tents and dismembering them in the darkness. Often their screams were heard by local natives, who believed the beasts to be the spirits of long-dead chiefs expressing their rage at the invasion of their land by the white man's iron snake. Understandably, the railway labourers mutinied; they only returned to work after the Indian Army colonel in charge of the project had tracked down the animals and then put their carcases on display for all to see.

In May 1899, an up-country railhead was established at Nairobi, the last station on the line before it mounted the steep gradient of the Kikuyu Escarpment. There, entirely by accident, the future capital of Kenya began to grow—a cluster of tents at first, then a series of shacks and wooden bungalows, then a church, a clubhouse and a handful of stone buildings with the Union Jack flying above. By the time the railway was terminated, two years later, at Lake Victoria—400 kilometres to the north-west—Nairobi was already the most important settlement along its length.

The Uganda Railway was the last great engineering feat of the Victorian era. The speed with which it was completed was remarkable; a parallel line built in German East Africa, begun three years earlier on the coast at Tanga, advanced at a much slower pace, taking more than twice as long to cover just 128 kilometres to Korogwe and Momba. Yet the Central Railway, too, was a great work; when finally finished in 1914, it was to stretch 1,252 kilometres to Kigoma, near Ujiji on Lake Tanganyika.

Britain took great pride in the construction of the Uganda Railway, but once the euphoria had subsided, the nation was faced with a vexing question: how to justify a project whose ultimate cost amounted to a staggering £5.5 million. The obvious answer was through agricultural exploitation, possibly by white settlers. Uganda, however, had a torrid climate and lake shores that were a breeding ground for tropical diseases. More significantly, its fertile southern and central regions were dominated by strong African kingdoms. It was therefore concluded that Uganda should remain basically a black man's country: a British protectorate administered where possible by

A CHRONOLOGY OF KEY EVENTS

c. 3.7 million years B.C. Earliest known ancestor of man, *Australopithecus afarensis*, inhabits the area of Laetoli in northern Tanzania.

c. 1.8 million years B.C. Tool-making *Homo habilis* ("handy man"), the first-known member of the genus *Homo* which gave rise to modern man, lives in Olduvai Gorge in northern Tanzania.

c. 1000 B.C. Stone Age farmers and herdsmen spread down the Great Rift Valley from Ethiopia into central Kenya and Tanzania.

c. 500 B.C.–100 A.D. Bantu-speaking migrants from the Congo Basin, bringing knowledge of iron-working, settle in East Africa.

c. 700–900 Arab traders begin settling along the East African coast. Important trading centres are established at Malindi, Mombasa (*above*) and Manda Island. Organization of the slave trade begins.

c. 1000 Islam becomes the dominant religion along the entire East African coast, marking the development of Swahili culture, a blend of African and Arab influences.

c. 1100 Arab and Persian merchants establish a powerful city on Kilwa Island, in southern Tanzania.

1300–1400 Four African kingdoms emerge in the area of modern Uganda: Toro, Ankole, Bunyoro and Buganda.

1498 Portuguese sailors under the command of Vasco da Gama become the first Europeans to reach East Africa by sea, stopping at Mombasa and Malindi.

1502 On a second voyage, Vasco da Gama compels the Sultan of Kilwa to pay tribute to the King of Portugal.

1505 A Portuguese fleet commanded by Francisco de Almeida sacks and burns the cities of Kilwa and Mombasa. By the end of the decade all the East African city-states have been brought under Portuguese hegemony.

1652 Responding to Swahili appeals for aid against the Portuguese, the Omanis send ships to Zanzibar and to Pate Island (off modern-day Kenya).

1840 Sayyid Said, Sultan of Oman and *de facto* ruler of most of the East African coast, transfers his capital from Muscat to Zanzibar. The slave trade develops on a major scale.

1841 Britain establishes a diplomatic mission in Zanzibar and strives in vain to end the slave trade.

1846–1849 German missionaries Johann Rebmann and Johann Krapf become the first Europeans to set eyes on Mount Kilimanjaro and Mount Kenya respectively.

1858 British explorers Richard Burton (*above*) and John Hanning Speke discover Lake Tanganyika; Speke goes on to locate and name Lake Victoria.

1866 Dar es Salaam is established by the Sultan of Zanzibar as a deep-water port and trading centre.

1871 Henry Morton Stanley finds the explorer-missionary Dr. David Livingstone at Ujiji, and together they explore the northerly end of Lake Tanganyika.

1884 German metaphysician Dr. Carl Peters forms the Society for German Colonization; his treaties with African chiefs in present-day Tanzania bring huge tracts of land under German control, starting the European "scramble for Africa".

1890 By the Heligoland Treaty, Germany recognizes British claims to Uganda, and Britain acknowledges the German presence south of a line that now marks the Kenya–Tanzania border. Zanzibar is established as a British protectorate.

1895 The Protectorate of British East Africa is proclaimed.

1895–1908 The British undertake a series of military campaigns against the Nandi of central Kenya; expeditions are mounted against the Embu and Kisii.

1896 Construction work begins on the Uganda Railway, linking Mombasa with Lake Victoria.

1899 Nairobi is founded as an up-country railhead on the Uganda Railway.

1905 Nairobi succeeds Mombasa as capital of British East Africa.

1905–1907 The Maji-Maji rebellion against German rule spreads throughout southern Tanganyika. It serves to unite disparate tribal groups against foreign domination, but at least 75,000 African lives are lost in vain.

1914 Soon after the outbreak of World War I, a British warship bombards Dar es Salaam in German East Africa. Four years of war between British and German forces follow.

1916 South African general J.C. Smuts is appointed commander-in-chief of Britain's 30,000-strong East African army (*soldier opposite*).

1921 The Young Kikuyu Association

(later renamed the Kikuyu Central Association) is founded to press for land rights and air labour grievances.

1922 German East Africa, renamed Tanganyika, is mandated to Britain by the League of Nations.

1928 Jomo Kenyatta becomes general secretary of the Kikuyu Central Association.

1944 The Kenya African Union (KAU) is formed; three years later Jomo Kenyatta becomes its president.

1950 The Kenyan government arrests African and Asian trade unionists, so provoking a general strike in Nairobi.

1952 The Mau Mau rebellion starts. Kenya governor Sir Evelyn Baring declares a state of emergency; Kenyatta and other black leaders are arrested. The Uganda National Congress (UNC) is founded.

1953–1956 Colonial forces wear down and defeat the Mau Mau uprising in the Kenya highlands.

1954 Julius Nyerere founds the Tanganyika African National Union (TANU), dedicated to achieving Independence from Britain.

1958 TANU sweeps the polls in a general election held in preparation for Independence.

1960 The Uganda People's Congress is founded by Milton Obote. The Kenya African National Union (KANU) is formed; Kenyatta becomes its leader after his release from a British prison the following year.

1961 Tanganyika wins Independence with Nyerere as Prime Minister, later President of the new government. On Zanzibar, anti-Arab rioting mars the general election.

1962 Uganda achieves Independence.

1963 Zanzibar celebrates Independence (*below*) with its sultan as head of state. Kenyatta leads Kenya to Independence. The Uganda Republic is established with Mutesa II, the Kabaka of Buganda, as President and Milton Obote as Prime Minister. The capital is moved from Entebbe to Kampala.

1964 Rebellion in Zanzibar overthrows the Sultan and leaves 5,000 Arabs dead. Zanzibar joins in a limited union with Tanganyika to form the United Republic of Tanzania.

1965 Tanzania becomes a one-party state.

1966 The Ugandan Prime Minister Obote becomes President after sending troops under Colonel Idi Amin to overthrow the Kabaka of Buganda. Kenya becomes a one-party state.

1967 Nyerere launches Tanzania's drive towards socialism with the Arusha Declaration. The governments of Tanzania, Kenya and Uganda set up the East African Community as a trading bloc.

1970–1975 Chinese engineers (*left*) build the Uhuru Railway across southern Tanzania, linking Dar es Salaam with Lusaka in Zambia.

1971 General Idi Amin deposes President Obote; the following year he expels 40,000 Asians from Uganda.

1977 Kenyatta seizes control of East African Airways, hastening the end of the East African Community and causing a rift with Tanzania.

1978 President Kenyatta dies and is succeeded by President Daniel arap Moi. An invasion by the Ugandan army of Tanzania's West Lake Province provokes a Tanzanian counter-invasion the next year which re-establishes a civilian government in Uganda.

1980 Obote returns from exile in Tanzania to become Uganda's Prime Minister and President for the second time.

1982 A coup attempt by air force officers in Kenya is crushed by the army; hundreds are killed in street battles, and the air force is disbanded.

1983 The Arusha Summit produces a three-power agreement for financial settlement of the disbanded East African Economic Community. Diplomatic relations between Kenya and Tanzania are resumed.

1985 General Tito Okello seizes Kampala, ousts President Obote and establishes a new military regime.

1986 The forces of the National Resistance Army overthrow Okello; Yoweri Museveni is installed as President of Uganda.

2

local kings or chiefs, and elsewhere (mainly in the north) by British district officers or newly appointed local authorities. The railway would simply be used to open up new markets and new crops for the region's farmers; in particular, it would transport cotton, which grew well in Uganda and would require little capital.

In contrast, Kenya, like German East Africa, had no tradition of strong centralized government. There, scores of different peoples lived shoulder to shoulder, each divided from the other by their own boundaries and loyalties. Large-scale agricultural development, it was argued, could only be made viable with a considerable degree of foreign control; and fortuitously Kenya, with its rich soil and bracing climate, was very well suited to farming by non-Africans. After toying with the idea of giving Kenya's undeveloped highlands to the Indian rail workers, or even to

East European Jews suffering persecution at home, the British government decided that the best solution was to encourage white men from all parts of the Empire to come and settle the land.

One of the first to answer the call was a reckless, quick-tempered young aristocrat named Lord Delamere. He had inherited vast estates in England while still a schoolboy at Eton, where he had distinguished himself only by losing £300 in a single bet at Ascot

At the dawn of the 20th century, the elegant British Residency, adorned with spears, guns and big-game trophies, was the true seat of power in Zanzibar. Although the Sultan retained nominal authority, Britain in practice exerted political and economic control over the island's affairs.

races. In Nairobi, he lived up to his reputation as a hellraiser by locking in a meat-safe a hotel manager who had asked him to leave his establishment, and by lighting a fire under a government building after some local bureaucrats had incurred his displeasure.

Happily, British East Africa was the making of Lord Delamere. Forced to sell his English estates after a series of financially disastrous agricultural experiments, he buckled down to the task of making his fortune in Africa. The trouble was that nobody knew what kind of farming would flourish in Kenya. The land he acquired in the Great Rift Valley was available because the Masai never grazed it. After several years of raising sheep and cattle he discovered that the grass was deficient in iron and other minerals. He thought it would at least be good for wheat, and so, at vast expense, he planted over a thousand hectares with a hardy Australian strain. Hopefully he watched it ripen, only to see it wither and die a few days short of harvesting, a victim of black-stem rust.

So it went on. By trial and error, often at enormous cost, Delamere and other pioneers slowly learnt which crops could be farmed with success—most notably maize, coffee and sisal. Fortunately for themselves and for the long-term development of the country, many of the early landowners had

Sir Hesketh Bell, the first British governor of Uganda, poses in 1908 with his administrators and the rulers of the long-established kingdoms of Buganda, Ankole, Toro and Bunyoro. In the centre is Daudi Chwa, the Kabaka of Buganda, whose father had been exiled to the Seychelles.

2

In April 1917, during the anti-German
offensive in World War I, a British
convoy pauses on a road near Mount
Kilimanjaro. Though outnumbered by
10 to one, the German forces—led by
General Lettow-Vorbeck, a master of
bush warfare—were never completely
defeated in battle.

capital to spare to fund agricultural experiments. Lord Hindlip and Lord Cranworth were among the pioneer farmers who retained large estates in England, as did Lord Enniskillen in Ireland; and the American Northrup McMillan was already a millionaire when he arrived from St. Louis.

Others, such as Ewart "Grogs" Grogan—a grandson of Prime Minister Gladstone—came with little ready cash but with tremendous energy and the determination to succeed. Grogan indeed was a man in the Delamere tradition: a young rebel who had first visited Africa after being sent down from Cambridge for locking a goat in a professor's room. Later, to prove his initiative to the demanding father of the girl he loved, he became the first man to walk the 7,000-plus kilometres from Cape Town to Cairo. Less commendably, he once killed a drunken Portuguese with a single punch, and over the years he fathered several illegitimate children by Africans. Nevertheless, Grogan was highly intelligent, a world authority on fiscal theory, and he eventually became one of white Kenya's most respected citizens.

At the time, however, Kenya's economic progress was achieved largely at the cost of the African population. They paid in blood, and in the loss of land, freedom and dignity. Backed up by military forces, the European colonists took over traditional tribal lands and imposed taxes aimed at forcing Africans to work for European farmers. Many tribes fought back, but they were hopelessly ill-equipped with only their spears and shields to resist foreigners armed with rifles and the Maxim machine gun.

Surprisingly, the Masai were not in the forefront of the resistance, largely because their semi-nomadic way of life was not immediately threatened. As pastoralists, they were judged to be unsuitable for labour on settlers' farms or on the administration's new road-building projects; also, they were not tied to any cultivated land.

In contrast, the Nandi of central Kenya were the target of a series of British campaigns between 1895 and 1908, which cost them more than 1,000 lives and many wounded, plus tens of thousands of sheep and cattle which were confiscated and, for the most part, handed over by the military to white settlers. In 1906, the Embu, also of central Kenya, suffered more than 400 losses in a British "punitive expedition". In 1908, the nearby Kisii tribe were ruthlessly punished for recalcitrance. After a hundred or more of them had been killed, an Under-Secretary of State at the Colonial Office in London (one Winston Spencer Churchill) was moved to send a cable of protest to the Governor of Kenya: "Surely, it cannot be necessary to go on killing these defenceless peoples on such an enormous scale?"

The fighting was both ruthless and bloody, and was justified by its defenders as the sharp edge of Britain's "civilizing mission" in Africa. A prominent leader of the "pacification" expeditions was Captain Richard Meinertzhagen of the 3rd Battalion of the King's African Rifles. In his journals, Captain Meinertzhagen recalls how he razed a Kikuyu village after the news reached him that a Kikuyu had murdered a white man, having pegged him down and then urinated in his mouth. "I have performed a most unpleasant duty today . . . I gave orders that every living thing except children be killed without mercy. Every soul was either shot or bayoneted . . . we systematically cleared the valley in which the village was situated, burnt all huts, and killed a few more niggers.''

Despite his harsh and racist attitudes, Meinertzhagen was one of the very few Europeans who anticipated the long-term folly of British policy in East Africa, and especially of the plans of High Commissioner Sir Charles Eliot to transform the central Kenya highlands of the Kikuyu into "white man's country". As early as 1902, he wrote that "the Kikuyu are ripe for trouble, and when they get educated and medicine men are replaced by political agitators there will be a general rising . . . I cannot see millions of educated Africans—as there will be in a hundred years' time—submitting tamely to white domination. After all, it is an African country, and they will demand domination. Then blood will be spilled, and I have little doubt about the eventual outcome.''

Further south, in present-day Tanzania, the Germans were dominating with no less ruthlessness. A number of tribes resisted heroically, most notably the Hehe under their king Mkwawa, and the Yao under Masemba. Indeed, Mkwawa proved such a formidable foe that, after his final defeat and suicide in 1895, the Germans severed his bullet-shattered head from his body and sent it back to the Reich to be preserved in Bremen's Anthropological Museum. (It can now be seen in the small memorial museum at Kalenga, Mkwawa's old fortified capital.)

It was in 1890 that the German commander, Hermann von Wissman, first demanded the surrender of the Yao. Chief Masemba replied in a letter: "I have listened to your words but can find no reason why I should obey you—I would rather die first. If it should be friendship that you desire, then I am ready for it, today and always, but your subject I cannot be. I am sultan here in my land. You are sultan there in yours. Yet listen: I do not say that you should obey me, for I know you are a free man. As for me, I will not come to you, and if you are strong enough, then come and fetch me.'' The Germans came, but it was another nine years before they finally overwhelmed the Yao.

By then, the German colony had been divided into 19 districts, each controlled by a virtually all-powerful white commissioner, and large estates of sisal, cotton, coffee and rubber were well established. The greatest cause of grievance was the German policy of forcing the people to work on plantations of cotton grown for export to Europe. The Africans laboured literally under the whip, and were paid absurdly low wages that barely met the tax demands made upon them by their

A DRAMATIC EXPANSION OF BRITISH RULE

As shown in the maps (*left*), the face of East Africa radically changed as a result of the defeat of Germany in World War I. In 1922, the League of Nations formally gave the bulk of German East Africa, renamed Tanganyika, the status of a mandated territory under British rule. The rest of the German colony— the small kingdoms of Rwanda and Burundi south of Uganda—was designated a Belgian mandate.

The wartime Protectorate of British East Africa (redesignated Kenya Colony in 1920) lost the north-eastern province of Jubaland to Italian Somaliland in 1925—a deal arising from secret arrangements that had brought Italy into the war on the Allies' side in 1916. Uganda, as before the war, remained a British protectorate.

BRITISH   EGYPTIAN   GERMAN   INDEPENDENT
BRITISH INFLUENCE   ITALIAN   PORTUGUESE

masters. It was a new form of slavery that served to unite the various peoples against a common enemy and resulted in the greatest mass uprising in Tanzania's history: the Maji-Maji rebellion of 1905 to 1907, a challenge to colonial power that cost 75,000 lives.

The rebellion began as a protest against forced labour on cotton plantations along the Rujifi river and escalated into a war throughout southern Tanganyika. Its name—Maji-Maji (Water! Water!)—derived from the fact that the African freedom fighters were persuaded by the teachings of prophet-like medicine-men that they could acquire immunity to bullets by drinking, or being anointed with, a sacred water. The strength of their belief was most dramatically demonstrated on August 30, 1905, when machine guns at the German fort of Mahenge rained death on thousands of rebels who, unflinchingly, advanced in wave after wave, armed only with sticks and spears.

Far and wide, the Maji-Maji insurgents attacked European settlements, farms, mining projects and mission stations, and at one time they even threatened to reach the capital of Dar es Salaam. But by October, three months after the rising began, the Germans were gaining the initiative and gradually driving the rebels into the bush by destroying their crops and cutting off food supplies.

For Africans, the rebellion, and the appalling famine that followed, served as the most devastating evidence of the futility of trying to drive out the white man by force. Yet it also set a significant precedent: for the first time disparate tribal groups, nine in all, had been united in action by their profound hatred of European rule.

For the sake of undisturbed farming operations, both British and German colonists after the outbreak of the rebellion sought to lure Africans into voluntary employment by offering improved inducements. In 1906, the British administration took a major step forward when it laid down minimum wage and ration levels for farm labourers. As Lord Lugard was to express it, Britain had a "dual mandate". "On the one hand, the abounding wealth of the tropical regions of the earth must be developed and used for the benefit of mankind; on the other hand, an obligation rests on the controlling Power not only to safeguard the material rights of the natives, but to promote their moral and educational progress."

But basically the attitude of Europeans in Africa remained unchanged. They still regarded the African as being little more than a savage who was fortunate to be benefiting from the white man's civilizing influence. Ewart Grogan echoed a fairly popular viewpoint when he wrote: "A good sound system of compulsory labour would do more to raise the nigger in five years than all the millions that had been sunk in missionary efforts for the past fifty . . . Let the native be compelled to work for many months in the year at a fixed and reasonable rate and call it compulsory education. . . . Under such a title, surely the most delicate British consciences may be at rest."

In practice, many of the settlers did little to set a civilizing example. There were regular Saturday night bar-room brawls and indiscriminate shooting of guns in the streets. In 1907, Kenya settlers publicly flogged three Nairobi rickshaw boys who were alleged to have behaved discourteously towards European women. In many ways, Nairobi and other similar settlements were like frontier towns of the American Wild West—a comparison which forcibly struck Theodore Roosevelt in 1909 when, after leaving the White House, he made his famous safari to British East Africa. He was wholly approving. "They were a fine set," he wrote, "these young Englishmen, whether dashing army officers or capable civilians. Moreover, I felt as if I knew most of them already, for they might have walked out of the pages of Kipling."

Roosevelt also noted that the British and the Germans were "doing in East Africa a work of worth to the whole world", and he expressed the hope that they would continue to operate there in thoroughly friendly rivalry. But, in the end, the two colonial powers proved to be as tribal as anyone. In Africa, they had taken the utmost care and diplomacy to avoid a fatal clash of interest, only to find themselves engulfed in the great conflict that exploded across Europe in 1914.

Under the 1885 Congo Act, the two administrations were entitled to remain neutral in the event of hostilities in Europe. Both sides, however, rightly feared the long-term consequences of a war between two European powers that employed African troops. As Heinrich Schnee, Governor of German East Africa, expressed it: "The prestige of the white man is at stake. If natives learn they can overcome white men in battle, it will give them ideas which will be dangerous for the future of all Europeans in Africa."

Possibly, though most improbably, a truce might have been established if a British navy cruiser had not bombarded the harbour of the German East African capital of Dar es Salaam in October 1914, thus provoking a series of retaliatory raids by the Germans

on the British railway in Kenya. Certainly neither side was ready for the confrontation when it finally came. In British East Africa there was just one battalion of the King's African Rifles, roughly 2,000 strong, to defend a frontier stretching from Lake Victoria all the way to the sea. The Germans' strength was only slightly greater.

The British, however, had the advantage of command of the Indian Ocean, and soon they received substantial reinforcements with the arrival of several shiploads of Indian troops hastily re-routed from other theatres of war. In November 1914, these Indian troops invaded the German port of Tanga—though not before the British commander had sportingly given the enemy 24 hours warning that the truce they had agreed earlier was no longer valid. The result was that the Germans, though outnumbered by approximately eight to one, were well prepared for the first night assault.

Britain's Indian troops were mostly raw recruits, unknown to their officers and still suffering from sea-sickness. They went straight into action over the side of landing craft, stepping into breast-high water and then struggling ashore through a mangrove swamp while German patrols fired at them in bright moonlight. Next morning, the British forces advanced through a swarm of African bees that delivered agonizing stings, and then ran into trip-wires fixed up with flags by the Germans to give the precise range for firing. The invasion was an appalling fiasco. When the British finally withdrew, they left behind them 800 dead and 500 wounded, also 16 machine guns, 455 rifles and 600,000 rounds of ammunition—just what the enemy desperately needed.

At Tanga, the *Schutztruppe*—African troops with German officers—were under the command of General Paul von Lettow-Vorbeck, who, like Rommel in World War II, was destined to become deeply respected by both British and Germans alike. Realizing that he could never hope to defeat the numerically superior forces ranged against him, he concentrated with extraordinary ingenuity on ways of making his own defeat impossible. The more British troops he could involve in will-o'-the-wisp hunts through the bush, the fewer there would be available for service in France and Belgium, the main theatres of war. His strategy worked brilliantly. By January 1916, more than 30,000 British Empire troops, aided by a large contingent of African volunteers, were tied up in scouring German East Africa for his relatively small guerrilla-style force. Although Lettow-Vorbeck never fought a pitched battle if he could avoid it, the British casualties were enormous—partly as a result of enemy action, but largely as a result of tropical diseases.

The longer Lettow-Vorbeck eluded them, the more the British troops admired him—and the more too they came to mistrust their own generals. Ironically, the hunting-down of the shadowy *Schutztruppe* only made significant progress after February 1916, when the South African J.C. Smuts, himself a former enemy of the British, was appointed commander-in-chief of the imperial army in East Africa. Here, at last, was one general who actually led British troops from the front; indeed, Smuts once rode so far forward on reconnaissance that he appeared in Lettow-Vorbeck's gunsights. The latter held his fire, as a gesture of respect for a worthy opponent.

By 1917, the operations of the *Schutztruppe* were severely restricted by lack of equipment. A bold attempt was made to supply them by a Zeppelin airship, which flew 3,000 kilometres from Bulgaria only to be turned back over the Sudan by the German Admiralty, which had false information of Lettow-Vorbeck's defeat. Thereafter they were compelled more and more to make use of natural resources. They tapped trees for rubber and made their own motor tyres by hand. They extracted paraffin from copra and quinine from cinchona bark. They even built a factory in the jungle to produce home-made ammunition. Gradually, though, they lost ground. They were forced back across the border into Portuguese Mozambique, and from there,

after months of guerrilla warfare, they made their way to Northern Rhodesia (present-day Zambia).

When the Armistice was declared in 1918, General Lettow-Vorbeck's forces were still in good heart, still ready to fight. Alone among Germany's armies, they had never suffered a significant defeat. Even so, their reluctant surrender signalled the end of German rule in Africa. In 1922, as part of the post-war peace settlement, German East Africa was mandated to Britain by the League of Nations on the understanding that it would be governed "in the interests of the native inhabitants". It was renamed Tanganyika.

After their defeat in World War I, the Germans were allowed to return to their farms in the newly established British colony of Tanganyika. But their old authoritarian system of administration was now replaced with "indirect rule", whereby British colonial officials exercised government through local chiefs.

By 1923, under this new regime, Tanganyika was paying its own way and no longer required grants-in-aid from the British government—an advance achieved initially by the extension of peasant cash-crop cultures such as cotton, coffee and tobacco, though later, in the 1930s, substantial European sisal plantations were organized. Similarly, in Uganda, the British government saw its main duty as one of maintaining an administration that could finance itself without subsidies from London. The peoples of Uganda were debarred from the ginning of cotton on the grounds that they were inefficient and might debase the product. Nonetheless, they were able to establish an expanding export market with-

out reducing the country to single-crop reliance, and without becoming subservient to European immigrants with demands for land and labour.

In contrast, the British government's immediate post-war aim in Kenya was to establish a more sizeable European community—one capable of farming on a large scale, and of providing formidable opposition in the event of a native uprising. Between 1902 and 1914, some 41,500 square kilometres of the finest land—a quarter of Kenya's arable territory—had been expropriated solely for European use. Now Britain encouraged white settlers to farm virgin lands in the far corners of the colony; and in Nairobi, the British colonial authorities held a grand draw at which two revolving drums took all day to parcel out land, virtually free, on 999-year leases.

This policy was bitterly contested by the Indian community, who outnumbered the whites by more than two to one, and who logically argued that land should be given to them as reward for their major contribution to the war effort. They also demanded political representation, which had been given to the whites in 1920, the year that the protectorate formally became Kenya Colony with a non-elective legislative council with powers that were purely advisory. Meanwhile, the European settlers were arguing that their own future should be made more secure by the creation of an elected legislative assembly in which they would have limited powers of law-making and government. In their view, electoral equality should be denied to the Indian minority, and Africans should have no voice at all.

By 1923, with tempers rising among Europeans and Indians, Whitehall fell

2

back on a compromise: the Indian minority would have five representatives in a newly enlarged legislative council in which the European settlers were guaranteed a dominant influence. On this council, the Africans—then numbering 2.5 million as opposed to 10,000 Europeans and 23,000 Indians—would be represented by just one European, appointed to act as a spokesman for their interests. Remarkably, these changes were contained in the so-called Devonshire White Paper of 1923 which also made the following important declaration: "Primarily, Kenya is an African territory, and H. M. Government think it necessary to record their considered opinion that the interests of the African natives must be paramount, and that if and when those interests and the interests of the immigrant races should conflict, the former should prevail."

In reality, however, this declaration merely served as a cover for continued and greatly enlarged European paramountcy. During the 1920s, British settlers flocked to the central highlands of Kenya in their hundreds—an extraordinary collection of people, the like of which had never been seen in the history of colonial expansion. Where emigrants to other parts of the British Empire were usually of middle or working class extraction, the Kenya settlers were more often aristocrats: men such as Ferdinand Cavendish-Bentinck, later Duke of Portland, and Lord Francis Scott, son of the Duke of Buccleuch. Significantly, too, the ex-servicemen among the settlers were predominantly drawn from the officer class—to such a degree that there was a popular saying at the time: "Officers to Kenya, N.C.O.s (non-commissioned officers) to Rhodesia." It was a pattern

that explains to a large extent the very different tone and style of white settlement in the two African countries: Kenya consciously upper-class, Rhodesia dourly middle-class.

The newcomers included an unusual number of eccentrics and pleasure-seeking opportunists. Among the more successful was Eric Sherbrooke Walker, a penniless Englishman who had fallen in love with the Earl of Denbigh's daughter and had earned the money to marry her by smuggling rum to America during Prohibition. Once in Kenya, he invested the proceeds in hotels—first *The Outspan*, where the founder of the Boy Scout movement, Lord Baden-Powell, was to live out his last years in the 1930s, then *Treetops*, where his descendants were to be hosts to Princess Elizabeth on the night in 1952 she became Queen of England.

Like most settlers of his time, Walker was an ex-soldier who, having survived the war to end all wars, was determined to enjoy the peace to the full. In the 1920s, when he arrived, Kenya had more than 3,000 European farmers, many of whom displayed an unbounded appetite for pleasurable pursuits. For the sporting, there was golf (with the unusual hazard of lions lurking in the rough on some courses), cricket, polo, tennis, horse-racing, pig-sticking (with wart hogs serving as the pigs), fishing in icy streams of the Aberdare mountains which had been stocked with trout from New Zealand, and even fox-hunting, with a jackal or a duiker serving as the fox. And for almost everyone, in the hedonistic Jazz Age, there was drinking, dancing and partying without end.

"Are you married, or do you live in Kenya?" became a British joke, reflecting the fact that, in Kenyan

Protected by strict anti-hunting laws, a herd of buffalo graze securely in Tanzania's Ngorongoro Crater Conservation Area. Fifty years ago, however, such big game was slaughtered on a massive scale by trophy-hunters on safari—among them the Duke of Gloucester (inset).

71

2

society, adultery seemed to be the rule rather than the exception. A notorious area in the central highlands became known popularly as Happy Valley. Here, one of the outstanding personalities was Lady Idina Sackville, who worked her way through five husbands, with numerous paramours in between. Guests at her house often took cocaine and tossed their bedroom keys into a hat before selecting their night partners at random.

Another outrageous society hostess was the beautiful American, Alice de Janze, who kept lion cubs in her home and who shot one of her lovers in the chest before taking her own life. She asked for a cocktail party to be held over her grave.

At one time or another, both women had been involved with Josslyn Hay, 22nd Earl of Erroll, the most notorious adulterer of them all. Promiscuous, spoiled and handsome, Lord Erroll was a charming, utterly selfish cad who had never done an honest day's work in his life. With scarcely a penny to his name, he survived largely by borrowing from the women he enticed into his bed. Other men's wives were always fair game for him, and other men's children were often welcomed by him with the words, "Come to Daddy".

In January 1941, the fast-living English peer was found slumped on the floor of his Buick with a bullet embedded in his skull. Innumerable men had good reason to exult over his death, but the chief suspect was a fellow Old Etonian, Sir Henry Delves Broughton, a wealthy old baronet with an attractive young wife. After two and a half months of marriage Lady Broughton had recently confessed to her husband that she had fallen in love with Joss Erroll; and it was from the Broughton house in Nairobi that Erroll was driving away on the night he was killed. The police drew the obvious conclusion, and Kenya's most sensational trial opened at the colony's Supreme Court the following May.

The police evidence hinged on a pair of Colt revolvers which Sir Delves had reported stolen just before the murder. They argued that one of these must have been the murder weapon, only to be outwitted by a brilliant defence lawyer who established that the murder had been committed by a five-grooved barrel with a right-hand twist, whereas all Colt 32 revolvers had a six-grooved barrel with a left-hand twist. The prosecution's case collapsed, and Sir Delves stepped from the dock a free man. He committed suicide soon afterwards, but not before confessing to a friend that he had indeed killed the Earl of Erroll, and had thrown the gun into the nearby Thika Falls. Whether he was telling the truth, or whether he simply wanted to take the credit for an exceedingly popular murder, no one will ever know.

The Erroll affair was seen at the time as the death knell of the Happy Valley set, but in reality that soft-living world had been in decline for more than a decade—ever since the Wall Street crash of 1929. In the early 1930s, the price of coffee, one of Kenya's main exports, had fallen by half, and then by half again, making it impossible for any but the most efficient farmers to operate at a profit. Tea, sugar and sisal had also plummeted in price, with particularly serious consequences for Uganda and Tanganyika. The recession made suicides of some European farmers, drunks of many more; and the freeloaders and so-called "Champagne Charlies" were among the first to leave East Africa and sail for home.

The people least affected by the Depression were the Africans, who had little to lose. In Kenya, for example, Africans had been forbidden to grow coffee lest the competition should put Europeans out of business. Thus, in the 1930s, they continued to exist much as they had always done, on a hand-to-mouth basis. But there was one important difference. Largely as a result of the education in mission-schools, a new generation of sophisticated and articulate Africans was emerging. And throughout the continent, a younger generation was seeking more advanced education abroad—men such as Jomo Kenyatta of Kenya, Hastings Banda of Nyasaland, Obafemi Awolowo of Nigeria, and Kwame Nkrumah of the Gold Coast.

More and more, too, the Africans were giving expression to their political grievances, and none more vehemently than the Kikuyu, who fairly argued that the best land in Kenya had been stolen from them. In 1932, a British Commission decided that some 260 square kilometres of territory had indeed been "accidentally" taken from the Kikuyu in the early days of colonization; and by way of compensation they granted them a rather larger, but less fertile area in the region of Nairobi. But this did not satisfy the Kikuyu. Nor did it please Kenyan Europeans, who proclaimed that they had delivered the Africans from tribal warfare and the slave trade, and who argued that the Kikuyu only wanted their land back once they had been shown how it could be exploited.

Herein lay a fundamental error on the white man's part: a failure to understand the Kikuyu's need for large

tracts of land left fallow so that they could move to them when the fertility of their cultivated land had been exhausted. The problem was summed up by the British anthropologist L. S. B. Leakey, who had grown up among the Kikuyu. In 1935, he wrote: "To the white man, bushland, as distinct from cultivated land and grassland, appeared to be unutilized land and many a settler who took up areas in the Kikuyu country in the early days holds firmly to the view that the land which

he took over was unoccupied and unused, because it was virgin bush. But to the African, virgin land is ideal pasturage for goats and sheep. The Kikuyu bushland was as much in use and occupation as the great grassland of the European stock owners today."

During the following decade, the Kikuyu were to become increasingly bitter over their loss of traditional territory—land on which they were now expected to labour as wage-employees of white owners. And that

bitterness became all the greater when many of them saw service overseas in World War II. They were told by British propagandists that the global conflict was *vita vya uhuru*, "the war for freedom", and that it was being fought because it was wrong for one tribe (the Germans) to seek domination over others. After the war was over, as Africans logically applied such reasoning to their own predicament, the *uhuru* call for independence began to echo far and wide across the continent.

A sleek dhow, used to travel to neighbouring islands, sails by the Zanzibar waterfront. In past centuries the town's harbour was packed with dhows from November to March, when monsoon winds and currents swept Indian and Arab traders south-westwards across the Indian Ocean.

THE ISLAND OF MEMORIES

Photographs by Christopher Pillitz

Zanzibar is a place of strong sensations. It seduces the visitor with the scent of its tropical spices, the colour of its flowers and fruits, the babble of different languages in the markets and the languid warmth of its equatorial sun. But the island is also haunted by memories, because no region in East Africa possesses so many reminders of its chequered past.

Its cosmopolitan heritage is most evident in Zanzibar town, a charming if decaying port built of mortar and coral taken from nearby reefs. Here, the variety of peoples drawn to the island is reflected in a mélange of Muslim mosques, Christian churches and Hindu temples, and in historic buildings put up by Portuguese invaders, Omani sultans and British colonial administrators. The cultural mix shows too in the faces and dress of the people—old men in white robes and embroidered caps or fezzes, young men in Persian-style winkle-pickers and women in colourful African prints.

Among so many souvenirs of the past, one historical institution has happily disappeared without trace. The slave market, where tens of thousands of men, women and children shipped over from the mainland were auctioned each year, was closed in 1873. It was replaced by an Anglican cathedral, whose altar is positioned precisely on the site of the old whipping block.

In the 19th century, Zanzibar's pivotal position off the East African coast favoured its development as the hub of an Arab trading empire. With its sister island of Pemba, about 40 kilometres to the north, it became the clove centre of the world and the most important entrepôt in the western Indian Ocean.

The corrugated-iron roofs of Zanzibar town spread out in front of the twin towers of St. Joseph's church, while in the foreground a pennant marks the triangular roof of a Hindu temple. Due to lack of money and little concern for restoration, many of the buildings have crumbled in the salt air.

On the Zanzibar waterfront, graceful
old palm trees flourish beside a row of
tenements that have fallen into decay.
The small boats moored by the shore
are used by the local residents to
augment their generally low incomes
with some fishing.

Zanzibar men, wearing the embroidered caps of coastal Muslims, watch two friends playing dominoes on an outdoor table.

A tailor sitting at a sewing machine outside his home in Zanzibar town stitches together a traditional cap for a Muslim customer.

Carrying food home from market, a woman passes a street trader who offers green bananas by the basketful.

In the courtyard of her house, a woman fries three-cornered sweetmeats to sell at Zanzibar's main market.

Within the carpeted precincts of a Zanzibar mosque, a worshipper— barefooted according to custom— stands quietly in prayer. Despite the presence of other faiths, the overwhelming majority of Zanzibaris are Muslims, and religious attitudes on the island tend to the puritanical.

In Zanzibar town, Muslim women in traditional dress stroll past a latticed veranda whose design reflects the island's Arab heritage.

3

The leaders who took the East African nations to Independence were cast in different political moulds. Kenya's Jomo Kenyatta *(left)* was a pragmatic conservative, Uganda's Milton Obote *(centre)* a determined manipulator, while Tanzania's Julius Nyerere *(right)* followed a socialist path.

THREE ROADS TO FREEDOM

When the guns of the Second World War fell silent, there were few signs to indicate that the end of colonialism in East Africa was in the offing. The war had apparently enhanced the financial prospects of the white farmers and businessmen, and they viewed the future with satisfaction. The farmlands of Europe had been devastated by more than five years of warfare, so export prices for agricultural products could be expected to remain high. In addition, East Africa's own economy was growing quickly. Local enterprises were now supplying goods and services which had previously been provided from Britain.

The white communities were also swelling in number. In Kenya they would grow from around 23,000 in 1939 to more than 29,000 by 1948; in Tanganyika from 8,000 to 10,500; and from 2,000 to 3,500 even in Uganda, where white settlement was no part of Britain's imperial plan. That these communities remained tiny in comparison with the size of the African populations—at least five million in Kenya, around seven million in Tanganyika and nearly five million in Uganda—appeared not to matter to the majority of settlers. Buttressed with the knowledge that the colonial government was behind them, they discounted all danger of an African revolt against themselves.

Most confident of all were the British farmers in Kenya, the wealthiest of all the settlers in East Africa. They numbered no more than 4,000 in the White Highlands, with smaller numbers scattered elsewhere. But in Kenya, uniquely amongst British colonies, government officials had been allowed to become landowners, which brought their personal long-term interests into line with those of the farmers. As they entered a new era of economic growth, these powerful allies looked forward to a day when they could strengthen their position still further, by winning dominion status within the British Commonwealth. Like Australia or Canada, they would then be released from the irritating constraints of the Colonial Office, personified by governors who had been appointed in London.

The officials' great ambition was to create another version of South Africa, centred on the White Highlands and the city of Nairobi. The three territories of Kenya, Uganda and Tanganyika would be joined together in a federation, with Europeans controlling the government, the economy and the armed forces. Where junior partners were required, whether as small traders or as clerks, the immigrant Asian communities, totalling about 200,000 in all three colonies, would fit the bill. They for the most part agreed that black Africans should remain at the lowest tier of all.

Independent white rule was not acceptable to the British government, however, and the settlers' dream was

3

never to materialize. But in Kenya especially, their power was real enough. The majority of whites felt and behaved like an aristocracy amongst serfs. Farmers and officials socialized together in exclusive clubs and handsome ranch-style houses, set within gardens bowered by flame trees and looking across lawns kept smooth and watered by voiceless black servants. Companions in the same enterprise, they exchanged the sundowner gossip of a world they felt was theirs to command, and one they thought they thoroughly understood.

They would soon find this secure world turned upside down, but the rumbles of upheaval had not gathered volume. As late as 1952, the provost of Nairobi Cathedral, the Reverend Hugh Hopkins, would try vainly to warn members of the local Rotary Club of the hatred the settlers aroused: "I do not think," he declared, "that we have any idea of the underlying dislike on the part of 95 per cent of the Africans for the Europeans."

The vast majority of European settlers in all three territories had indeed forgotten the bitter struggles of the colonial invasion; and African protests since then had been firmly suppressed. Those Africans who did manage to speak up in English were dismissed as troublemakers or "bad hats", and all their attempts at agitation were ruthlessly silenced. Colonial legislation had confined local politics to tribal welfare associations and more recently trade unions, formed by workers in the civil service, transport and the docks. But during the war all African politics had been banned.

Then the army veterans came home from their victories abroad. Of 200,000 East Africans demobilized by Britain, about half had seen active service: against the Italians in Somalia and Ethiopia—where they had restored a black emperor, Haile Selassie, to his throne; against the Germans in the Western Desert; or against the Japanese in Burma. They returned with a new confidence in their own abilities.

As one veteran expressed their mood, "We saw that, given a rifle, we could be better than a European." And they demanded to be rewarded for their loyalty during the Second World War. At open-air meetings with as many as 10,000 veterans in attendance, speaker after speaker called for a better deal for the Africans.

Almost without warning, the politics of nationalism strode to the centre of the stage. In all three colonies, Africans were inspired by the message of the black American leader, Marcus Garvey, whose speeches calling for Negro pride, unity and action had filtered across the Atlantic; and in July 1945 they also received encouraging reports of a more sympathetic government in Britain, where the socialist Labour Party had won a surprise victory over Winston Churchill's Conservatives. When news followed that India would now move towards freedom, East Africans too set their sights on their own independence.

But any hopes that freedom could be theirs for the asking were soon dashed. The Labour politicians, though committed in principle to self-government for the colonies, saw development, not independence, as the way forward. Governors might be allowed to appoint Africans to their ruling legislative council, but to grant sovereignty at this stage was thought to be, in the words of one cabinet minister, "like giving a child of ten a latch-key, a bank account and a shot-gun".

In the face of such a hesitant commitment to reform, not even the most confident African politicians expected East Africa would win independence quickly. A delay of 25, even 50, years seemed likely, in view of the forces ranged against them. But while thousands of new immigrants were still arriving from Europe, the demands for change were growing louder; and in Kenya, where the power of the colonists seemed strongest, a full-scale rebellion was about to erupt.

There was much at stake in Kenya for the British government. From humble beginnings as a row of army tents, Nairobi had become an administrative and communications centre that was vastly more developed than either Dar es Salaam or Kampala, and Mombasa was now an important naval base and supply port. Kenya was the centrepiece of British East Africa, and its settlers and colonial officials could be relied on to oppose any concession to the black majority. But the Africans, particularly the Kikuyu, were prepared to fight for freedom; the fierceness of their struggle would convince the British government that colonialism must depart from Kenya—and from Uganda and Tanganyika as well.

For Kenyan Africans, a portent of this change came in October 1946, when Jomo Kenyatta—who had been voluntarily in exile for 17 years—stepped off the train at Nairobi station and was given a hero's welcome. A burly, flamboyant man who had a penchant for good clothes—Kenyatta's adopted surname was the Kikuyu word for an elaborate belt—he was acknowledged as a leader by all of Kenya's African politicians.

Born into a typical peasant family, he had grown up in the first years of colonialism, and had been in contact with the British for most of his life. As a boy he attended a Church of Scotland mission; as a young man in Nairobi just after the First World War he had worked as a meter reader for the water authorities. But he played no part in the first stirrings of African politics. In

Watched by a British officer, NCOs of the King's African Rifles issue uniforms to Kenyan recruits to the regiment's Junior Leader Company. The company was set up just before Independence to train officers and technicians for the new national army.

3

fact, he was better known for his taste for the good life, and was soon running a bar and general store outside Nairobi which attracted a lively clientele from all over the country. By 1925 he was married, and doing well.

But in British East Africa there was a rigid limit to African advancement, and Kenyatta was soon chafing against it. His intelligence and gregariousness made him an obvious candidate for political involvement. In 1928 he was persuaded to become general secretary of the Kikuyu Central Association, which was then urgently seeking to curtail the loss of land to white settlement and to gain an education for Kikuyu children.

Kenyatta demanded a salary of one pound a day and a motorcycle, on which he soon became a familiar sight, driving around the dusty tracks of Kikuyuland to consult with the elders. But when he attempted to negotiate land rights for his people with the British colonial authorities, his demands were treated with Olympian disdain. In 1929 he sailed to Britain to lobby the Colonial Office directly.

Although his efforts were virtually ignored there too, Kenyatta remained in England, eventually becoming a student at London University. To raise money, he played an African chief in Alexander Korda's film *Sanders of the River*, and was bitterly criticized for this "degrading" role by other African exiles. But Kenyatta was undaunted. He lived his life as he wanted to, regardless of any dogma or convention. Always ready to enjoy himself, he made a wide circle of English friends, many of them well off, and attracted many female admirers. During the war years, which he spent in the Sussex countryside, he married an English-woman who soon bore him a son, although he made no secret of the fact that he would eventually return to Africa and leave her in England.

Despite such diversions, however, Kenyatta continued to promote the African cause throughout his stay in England. In 1938 he had published his university thesis on the Kikuyu people under the title "Facing Mount Kenya". Seven years later, he helped to organize a Pan African Congress in Manchester with W.E.B. Dubois of the United States and Kwame Nkrumah of Ghana.

Fifty-five years old at the time of his return shortly after the war's end, Kenyatta built himself a house, took two new wives, and plunged back into the mainstream of politics. With the wartime ban on African political activity lifted at last, the Kikuyu Central Association had developed into a nationalist movement, the Kenya African Union (KAU), calling for a wide range of reforms, and in June 1947 Kenyatta became its president. But the colonial governments had little time for black politicians. Kenyatta and his allies were paid little heed until, as a result of pressure from the settlers, the bannings and prohibitions began again.

In 1950, the government arrested several black trade unionists for serving as officers of a new and still illegal East Africa Trades Union Congress. These arrests provoked a general strike of black workers in Nairobi, to which the government replied with a show of force. Police and troops with armoured cars were deployed, and the strikers were buzzed by military aircraft.

Kenyatta had opposed this strike. Many of the more conservative African leaders, Kikuyu chiefs among them, were alarmed by militant unionism, and he was anxious to maintain their support. But the fires of nationalism had now been lit. Under pressure from the radicals, KAU demanded complete independence from Britain. The time for talking was over and the time for fighting was shortly to begin.

"Kenyan nationalism turned violent," wrote the Luo leader Jaramogi Oginga Odinga in 1967, "because for 30 years it was treated as seditious and denied all legitimate outlet." But the roots of violence lay deeper still in the scarcity of land, which was particularly severe amongst the Kikuyu of the central highlands. The colonial government had seized much of their ancestral terrain, and confined them to a reserve too small to support a growing population. For several decades, previously independent Kikuyu farmers had been driven into wage labour on white farms, or else into semi-legal squatting, tolerated by white farmers on the excess lands they possessed but did not use.

Other Kikuyus had fled from rural hunger to the slums and misery of Nairobi, where there was at least a chance that a man on his own could earn a wage or steal a living, while a woman, if so driven, could become a prostitute; and many did. Social conditions around the city, where Kikuyus far outnumbered other Africans, had descended into hopeless squalor. In 1953, an official enquiry found that most black workers in Nairobi could not pay for "accommodation which is adequate to any standard", and countless thousands slept on the streets. Since most were men who had left their families in the country, drunkenness and venereal diseases were rife.

The urban people who were dispossessed made willing recruits for the

HARSH MEASURES TO DEFEAT A BLOODY UPRISING

Suspected Mau Mau supporters huddle under guard in a detention camp set up by the British Kenyan government.

In October 1952, British rule in Kenya was threatened by a violent campaign of assassination and sabotage by Mau Mau terrorists, most of them from the Kikuyu region near Nairobi. The colonial government responded with a series of draconian counter-measures that led to four years of military operations against the rebels.

The security forces began their campaign by rounding up more than 20,000 Kikuyu suspects and confining them in detention camps. These captives were interrogated, and in some cases beaten and tortured. At the same time rebel strongholds in Kikuyuland were evacuated and declared "prohibited areas" in which Africans could be shot on sight.

When these measures failed to crush the rebellion, the military campaign was stepped up. In the course of Operation Anvil, launched in April 1954, a further 30,000 Kikuyus were removed to detention camps and Kikuyuland was sealed off from the rest of Kenya. These measures effectively ended the Mau Mau threat, and by 1956 the fighting was largely over.

Much publicity was given at the time to white victims of Mau Mau atrocities, but the overwhelming majority of casualties were Kikuyus. More than 13,000 Africans died during the uprising, victims either of the Mau Mau or the security forces.

Watchtowers and barbed wire surround the tents of the detention camp at Nyeri, where Kikuyus were held for interrogation.

Hooded in sacks to conceal their identities, two informers arrive at a detention camp to point out Mau Mau members and sympathizers.

An African guard removes the handcuffs from prisoners charged with the murder of a British farmer and two of his Kenyan servants.

3

guerrilla organization known mysteriously as Mau Mau, which suddenly emerged amongst the Kikuyu. During 1952, hundreds of men took an oath of loyalty; in August news reached Nairobi that the Mau Mau leaders were administering the oath of war. Standing naked and holding a ball of soil against his stomach, each warrior repeated:
"I speak true and swear before God and all present here
And by this Batuni Oath of the Movement
Which is called the oath of killing,
That if called upon to fight for our land,
To shed my blood for it,
I shall obey and never surrender."

So began a campaign of terrorism and sabotage that spread with the ferocity of a bush fire through Kikuyu country, although nowhere else save among neighbouring Embu and Meru tribes. Fearing the outcome, most other Kenyan peoples either remained neutral or backed the colonial forces. Even the Kikuyu themselves were divided about it. Pro-government chiefs condemned the rebels, and Kenyatta was persuaded diplomatically to denounce them as a dangerous menace. "Mau Mau has spoiled the country," he declared. "All people should search for Mau Mau and kill it."

Few Kenyans, black or white, believed in the sincerity of Kenyatta's anti-Mau Mau pronouncements, even though there was little evidence of his direct complicity in the movement. The settlers moved quickly to counterattack. Convinced that the guerrillas would seek to kill every European in the country, but at the same time entirely opposed to the least concession to African grievances, they besieged their new governor Sir Evelyn Baring,

a mild, patrician character who was no hawk by nature, with a clamour for severe action. Prosecuting oath givers and takers was not enough, they claimed; Kenyatta—the most conspicuous black nationalist leader in the country, whatever his stated views of the Mau Mau—must be arrested and the rebellion crushed with an iron fist.

Baring gave way to them. In October 1952, shortly after a prominent pro-government Kikuyu, Chief Waruhiu, had been shot down by a gunman 10 kilometres from Nairobi, he reluctantly declared a state of emergency. Kenyatta and 98 other black leaders were consigned to detention in a remote village of the far north, to await trial as organizers of Mau Mau. Baring went on to clear Nairobi of its Kikuyu inhabitants, now numbering more than 30,000, and ordered the entire population of the Kikuyu reserve to be confined within fortified settlements guarded by police.

The great rebellion eventually tore down every fixed opinion and belief, and destroyed on either side all barriers of mercy and restraint. By 1956, when it was over, an apparently invulnerable settler power found itself broken, yet in the aftermath nobody could agree on why and how all this had taken place. There were those among the whites who suspected a plot laid abroad, probably in Moscow, but that view never gained much credibility; the evidence pointed to local origins in central Kenya, where all the fighting took place. Others continued to put the blame on Kenyatta, described by a subsequent governor of Kenya as "the leader to darkness and death".

In December 1952, Jomo Kenyatta was brought to trial for allegedly "managing the Mau Mau terrorist

A Kenyan votes at a rural polling
station during the general election held
in 1963, shortly before Independence,
to choose a new national government.
The decisive winner was the Kenya
African National Union headed by
Jomo Kenyatta, who became the
country's first President.

3

organization". Although he continued to deny all guilt, he was convicted and sentenced to seven years' hard labour. In fact he was to spend the next eight and a half years in detention, only winning his release when the struggle for his country's independence had finally been won.

Meanwhile, the chain of violence and counter-violence was rapidly unwinding. In January 1953, police at Fort Hall in the Kikuyu reserve fired into a turbulent crowd and left 25 Africans dead. A few weeks later, Mau Mau guerrillas armed with machetes broke into an isolated farmhouse and butchered its owner and his wife, a young English couple named Ruck, together with their six-year-old child. Seven Kikuyu men were captured and hanged for their brutal killings. But the white community was not appeased. It had called for repression at the first signs of Mau Mau guerrillas; now it was calling for blood. In the middle of Nairobi, the verandas of the Norfolk Hotel saw angry meetings of settlers toting guns and talking of the urgent need to use them.

On the night of March 27, 1953, a Mau Mau band of about 3,000 axe-wielding guerrillas raided the pro-government Kikuyu village of Lari, not far from the capital, set houses on fire and massacred the chief and all his family. According to rebel sympathizers, police and settlers then counterattacked the following morning, killing even more villagers; and by the time peace was restored, more than one hundred men, women and children had been killed. That same night another Mau Mau band stormed a police post at Naivasha in the White Highlands and seized 47 weapons, including 18 sub-machine-guns with 3,780 rounds of ammunition. As though at a signal for insurrection, thousands of young guerrillas hurried to the dense bamboo forests of the Aberdare Mountains and the slopes of Mount Kenya, the natural bastions of Kikuyuland, where the Mau Mau leaders had their principal camps.

Organized in numerous separate groups called Land and Freedom Armies, the rebels in the Aberdares held out for more than three years; those of Mount Kenya, fewer and less well led, survived for almost as long. Practically unarmed at the outset, they stole their weapons from settler households or seized them from police and troops. Their actions at first were directed mainly against "loyal" Kikuyu and mission stations, but soon the guerrillas were involved in a full-scale war with the security forces.

As the military increased the pressure, the violence escalated sharply. The guerrillas stepped up their terror tactics, and they slaughtered their victims with the utmost savagery. The security forces—whose rapidly expanding ranks included professional thugs as well as loyalists—replied in kind. A wave of killing swept across Kikuyuland, but when bombers began pounding the guerrillas from the air, the rebels realized that their main goal must be survival; any positive action was beyond their power. Great forces were brought against them: 100,000 troops, including British and African military units, armed police and African militias, saw action before the rebellion came to an end.

However their motives and actions may be judged, the guerrillas' achievements in the face of such odds were impressive. Isolated in their forests, they were forced to fall back on their own resources, and responded with imagination. Two leaders emerged in the Aberdares: Dedan Kimathi, a man in his early thirties without family or education, and the slightly younger Karari Njama, a teacher who was one of a handful of literate men among the rebels. As Kimathi struggled to build unity of action among the various armies, Njama became secretary of a "Kenya Parliament" in the mountains, through which—as he intended—the rebels' aims of winning land and freedom were disseminated.

By the end of 1955, the rebels were on the run, and with the capture of Kimathi in October 1956, the Land and Freedom Armies were militarily defeated. Yet the political repercussions of their long campaign were profound, because the high cost of suppressing the revolt, both in African lives and British money, convinced the British government that independence must be granted quickly.

Only 32 white settlers lost their lives in the rebellion, but the black dead—including Mau Mau, security forces and innocent bystanders—reached the appalling figure of 13,000; and there was terrible suffering for many who did not die. When the financial figures were counted, taxpayers in Britain found they had to foot a bill for £60 million to protect a white settler system which was far from popular. Still more decisively, the white business community in Nairobi—and indeed some of the liberal farmers—reached the conclusion that any further attempts to strengthen white supremacy must now exclude all hope of a prosperous future. Business would do better in partnership with Africans.

The British government in London reached much the same conclusion and

turned away from the inflexible position of earlier years. In 1960 a new colonial secretary, the Conservative Iain MacLeod, finally conceded what the Land and Freedom Armies had taken to the hills to obtain. He negotiated a compensation scheme to give European estates back to Africans, allowed national political parties to be formed and announced that independence would soon be granted.

In August 1961, Kenyatta was freed by the governor of Kenya, Sir Patrick Renison. Two months later he was interviewed on British television, clasping the ebony stick that would become his trademark and wearing a Luo hat to emphasize his commitment to national unity. For whites as well as blacks, he had now become the obvious future leader of the country; and Kenyatta lost no time in asserting his authority and skills as President of the new Kenya African National Union (KANU).

When he declared himself willing to maintain close ties with Britain, and to support a multiracial, free-enterprise economy in return for a peaceful transfer of power, the final steps to freedom were quickly taken.

On December 12, 1963, the Duke of Edinburgh presented Kenyatta with the deeds of Independence at a ceremony in a specially built stadium in the capital Nairobi. The day passed with speeches, marching displays, mu-

Supporters of the Kabaka of Buganda, traditional ruler of the Ganda people, display their allegiance during Uganda's Independence celebrations. The Kabaka became President in Uganda's first national government, but was deposed four years later by the Prime Minister, Milton Obote.

sic and dancing. The festivities were attended by thousands of guests, including Kenyatta's English wife, who had flown out from London to join her African co-wives at the celebrations. At midnight, spotlights picked out the flag pole as the British flag was lowered for the last time; and as fireworks burst into the night sky, the new Kenyan standard rose proudly to take its place.

Events in Kenya may have set the pace for East African independence, but Kenya itself was the last of the region's

nations to attain that goal. First there was Tanganyika, which completed the course to national sovereignty almost two years before the Nairobi celebrations. In contrast to Kenya, Tanganyika's path to freedom was peaceful. One reason was that Britain was less committed to this Trust Territory, which it administered on behalf of the United Nations. But Tanganyika was also fortunate in producing a leader whose authority was scarcely questioned from the earliest days of the freedom movement until he resigned as President more than 30 years later.

Julius Kambarage Nyerere was born in 1922, near Musoma on the shores of Lake Victoria. His father was a government-appointed chief of the Zanaki people. Julius was educated at a Catholic mission and became one of the first Zanaki to convert to the faith, before moving to Makerere College in Uganda for higher education. Later he travelled to Scotland, where he took an arts degree at Edinburgh University, and at one time contemplated studying for holy orders.

Deciding instead to devote himself to the service of his country, Nyerere returned to Tanganyika and married a young woman from his own region. The couple built a house in Nyerere's village, for which the groom mixed the sand and cement with his own bare feet. (Thirty-five years later they would retire to the same modest home.) In 1952, Nyerere became a schoolmaster, working near Dar es Salaam. He then turned to public affairs and joined the Tanganyika African Association (TAA), a mainly town-based organization which sought to represent African interests to the colonial government. In 1953, at the age of 31, he was elected the movement's president.

A slim, diffident man who usually dressed in a white shirt, shorts and socks, Nyerere in those early days seemed an unlikely leader. But he was extremely determined, and a talented campaigner and political theoretician. He soon earned the title given to him by his followers: *Mwalimu*, the Swahili word for teacher.

Nyerere's organizing skills were tested to the full in the vast mainland of Tanganyika, where widely scattered populations and a dearth of road and rail transport posed huge obstacles to political unity. There were, however, two encouraging factors. Most people in Tanganyika spoke or understood Swahili, making communication easy; and no single group possessed the strength or even the ambition to aim, like the Ganda in Uganda or the Kikuyu in Kenya, at winning the lion's share of power.

The coffee-growing Chagga of Kilimanjaro might have regional strength, as did the cotton planters of lakeside Sukumaland and the traders and sisal farmers of the Tanga coast. However, neither they nor their neighbours were able to muster the manpower or poli-tical influence to dominate the whole country. In the long struggle for independence, the pull of local loyalties proved to be weaker than the call for united action.

On the other hand, Nyerere and the nationalists had few burning issues with which to arouse public resistance to colonial rule. The settler community in Tanganyika was fragmented. Although there were more than 10,000 European settlers in 1948, and almost twice that number in 1961, only a fraction of these were British, because—in keeping with the League of Nations mandate under which Britain first acquired the country—immigration had been open since the First World War to Europeans of all nationalities. The whites, including British, Germans, Greeks and South Africans, were split into several small communities. Immigrant Asians numbered about 46,000 in 1948, but they were led by men who saw clearly that the future lay in support for African nationalism.

Resentment of British rule was also relatively mild because, although the British liked to regard Tanganyika as one of their imperial estates, colonial development—and the attendant disruption of the local economy—had been practically nil. But there was one glaring example of economic folly.

Immediately after the war, there was a worldwide shortage of oils and fats. Consequently, in 1946, Tanganyika's white Director of Agriculture invited the Unilever company to set up a plantation to produce groundnuts for vegetable oil. Unilever declined, but the offer was quickly taken up by Britain's Ministry of Food, which decided to cultivate a million hectares of land. A government agriculturalist made a six-week aerial survey of the bush, then chose a vast area around Kongwa, on the central railway, where no one was living and the tree cover looked sparse, to grow the nuts. The entire scheme was conducted like a military operation, using bulldozers and converted tanks to clear the ground.

By 1950 a sum of £35 million had been invested—equalling the colonial government's entire expenditure for the same five-year period—but the groundnut scheme produced not one penny of profit. The land chosen was so dry and hard that it resisted the heaviest machinery. In 1947 a mere 3,000 hectares were cleared; in 1948 only 20,000; and in 1949 a severe drought withered the crops before they ripened. In 1950 the scheme was abandoned, with far more groundnuts having been planted as seed than were ever harvested.

The groundnut fiasco gave bite to Nyerere's demands for the British to withdraw. However, the nationalists' main task was to harness the tribal associations representing local interests around the country into a concerted national organization. Nyerere sought primarily to modernize and strengthen the TAA, whose voice was initially timid and ineffective. Something more forceful and above all more political was required.

In 1954, Nyerere and his allies established the Tanganyika African National Union (TANU) as a mouthpiece for the new, more determined nationalism. TANU aimed to draw the widest possible mass of people into the politics of independence. Many individual leaders worked for this goal. Men such as Rashidi Kawawa gave an impetus to peasant participation. In the capital, a Swahili woman trader, Bibi Titi Muhamed, recruited the women who traditionally brewed the beer sold in the markets into a women's section of TANU; and this women's movement spread across the country with the slogan "Unity is not for men alone". By 1958, TANU had some 300,000 listed members and by 1960 the figure had passed one million, or about one in five of all the adults in the country.

The British at first paid little heed to TANU. The governor of Tanganyika, Sir Edward Twining, regarded the leaders of TANU as an unimportant nuisance, and preferred to deal with the Africans he had appointed to his own legislative council. As late as 1957, when Independence was a foregone conclusion, Twining confided to a visiting official that he had told his senior administrators to avoid contact with Nyerere, describing him as "a bit of a trouble-maker, I think".

But only 18 months later, in September 1958, TANU swept the polls in a general election arranged by the colonial administration to produce a national government in the run-up to Independence. This decisive success stemmed from the party's ability not only to channel the aspirations of African communities, but also to win the support of both Europeans and Asians. Twining had proposed a "multiracial" system, by which he meant separate political representation for black, Asian and white Tanganyikans. But Nyerere and his companions would have none of it. Instead, they invited Europeans and Asians to join them in a common future.

Several strong personalities accepted Nyerere's invitation, notably a British farmer called Derek Bryceson and an Asian businessman, Amir Habab Jamal, who traded extensively with

At midnight on Independence Day, December 8, 1961, an army lieutenant raises the new Tanganyikan national flag on the summit of Mt. Kilimanjaro. At the same moment, a 75,000-strong crowd in Dar es Salaam cheered as the green, black and gold colours replaced the British standard.

India. Support for multiracialism withered, and Nyerere became the incontestable leader of Tanganyika. Appointed Prime Minister in May 1961, the so-called "trouble-maker" led his country to full constitutional sovereignty at midnight on December 8, 1961. By that time Twining had returned to Britain.

However, as mainland Tanganyika steered a safe course to freedom, the storms of racial violence were about to break in the Protectorate of Zanzibar, where the last of the Arab sultans was still on the throne. When Britain decided to withdraw from the island, in line with its general policy for East Africa, the dominant Arab community of 50,000, together with 20,000 immigrant Asians, thought they could remain in power. But the local Africans, whether long-term residents or lately arrived mainlanders, numbered about 230,000, and they had no intention of remaining subject to Arab landowners and traders. Anti-Arab rioting accompanied a general election in 1961, and when an Arab-led coalition won a hotly disputed victory, the mob went on the rampage. Sixty-eight Arabs were killed and 400 injured.

Much worse followed on January 12, 1964, just 33 days after Zanzibar acceded to Independence. A Ugandan immigrant named John Okello led an insurrection of the underdogs. Armed with only bows and arrows, axes and spears, his men routed the police and seized guns from their armoury before capturing the local radio station and calling for a mass uprising. As the Sultan fled the island in his private yacht, the African population fell on their oppressors; in all 5,000 Arabs were slaughtered. In the following few days, hundreds more Arab families were bundled into dhows and pushed out into the ocean.

Okello proclaimed himself field marshal, but within a fortnight his revolution had been taken over by the Afro-Shirazi Party, the largest of the African groups. Its leader, Abeid Karume, became president of a new Revolutionary Council with the support of the socialist Umma party. Okello himself returned to the mainland, and disappeared from public view.

Zanzibar now turned for aid to the East Germans and Chinese, arousing fears in the West that the island could become "the Cuba of Africa". With Umma demanding even more radical policies, the President turned to Nyerere for support. The price was a constitutional union between the countries, agreed in April 1964. Thus, after more than 250 years as an Arab sultanate, Zanzibar was reunited with the mainland, and its isolation gradually eased within the new United Republic of Tanzania.

In Uganda, the storms of violence and unrest would not break for several years after Independence, when fear and anger would spread uncontrollably across the rich farm lands, bringing ruin in their wake. Although the lead-up to Independence had involved prolonged wrangling among rival tribes and kingdoms, it was generally peaceful. There was not the bitter hatred between whites and blacks that had caused such bloodshed in Kenya or the African-Arab antagonism that had bedevilled Zanzibar.

British rule, it is true, was unpopular. Africans resented the colonial ban which prevented them from ginning their own cotton, and felt a powerful grievance against the Asian and European immigrants they had to pay to perform the operation. But the divisions among Africans, dating back to the earliest days of colonial conquest and beyond, provoked far more potent hatreds. When the new currents of political ambition began to flow with the end of the Second World War, these ancient rivalries were then cruelly exposed.

More than 50,000 demobilized servicemen brought the vision of freedom to Uganda in 1945. But when political parties were formed, each spoke for regional or sectional interests rather than for the nation as a whole. The fiercest divisions were between Protestant and Catholic Christians, and between the northern peoples and the central and southern kingdoms. The notion of a national unity simply failed to develop; Uganda might exist on maps and in law books, but scarcely at all in the minds of the Africans who were soon to inherit it.

A spirit of self-seeking amongst politicians made matters even worse, and divided the leaders from the led. Many had outstanding talents, but almost all regarded politics as a route to financial gain and superior status. The pursuit of national freedom was conducted in an atmosphere of sharp personal rivalry. As the politicians manoeuvred for power and privilege in Kampala, their links with the farmers at work in the fields and the herdsmen grazing their cattle grew steadily weaker.

A further divisive trend had appeared in Uganda's army. The British had recruited most of the troops from the Acholi, the Lango and their neighbours in the north of the country. By the time Independence was granted in 1962, the army had few southerners in its ranks, and only two officers were

African—one of them a heavyweight boxing champion named Idi Amin. Neither had any experience of command, nor any grasp of what national loyalties must mean if the army was to serve the cause of unity.

Of all the deep divisions, the most dangerous was that between the kingdom of Buganda and the rest of the country. In 1950 Buganda had a population of little more than three quarters of a million, while its people, the Ganda, were only one of 21 important groupings in the country. But Buganda's alliance with the incoming British around the turn of the century had given this kingdom an edge in political influence over all its rivals, and the Ganda had subsequently reinforced their position in business, education and politics. Their hereditary monarch, the Kabaka Sir Frederick Mutesa II, was determined that Buganda should retain its special privileges.

The British Governor in the run-up to Buganda's Independence was Sir Andrew Cohen, a masterful proconsular figure of wide experience, imposing self-assurance and commanding physique. Cohen tried hard to create some national unity before Britain's departure, and to reconcile Buganda with the other regions. In 1953, when Buganda rejected his design for the new nation, Cohen even banished the Kabaka to Britain for a while. A compromise was reached later in 1961 by which "King Freddie" would become a non-executive president of indepen-

dent Uganda, and there would be 21 Ganda representatives in a patched-up national assembly of 82 members. In the long term, however, Cohen's solution failed; and the man destined to succeed him in the seat of power, Uganda's first Prime Minister Milton Apollo Obote, inherited problems he would prove unable to solve.

Born in 1924 in Uganda's northern plains, Obote had risen from humble origins as the son of a Lango farmer to win a prominent place in East African nationalist politics. After studying at Makerere University, he moved to Kenya where he worked as a salesman and became a founding member of the Kenya African Union. On his return to Uganda in 1957, he was nominated to the country's legislative council, and became leader of the Uganda National Congress. Under Obote's calculating direction, this party responded like a chameleon to the shifts in the balance of influence among Uganda's several nationalist parties.

In 1960, Obote's own faction renamed itself the Uganda People's Congress. Two years later, the UPC won a comfortable majority in nationwide elections to the legislative council. On October 9, 1962, Obote led Uganda to full Independence as the nation's first Prime Minister. Considering his experience and parliamentary skill, he might have been expected to succeed in national unity, but the divisions within the nation proved impossible for him to try and resolve.

A man of little charisma but powerful will, Obote used every means at his disposal—cabinet reshuffles, changes in the governing coalition, constitutional revisions, concessions or threats to the rival local interests—in order to bully the warring politicians and re-calcitrant kings and chiefs into accepting the authority of his government. But within four years of Independence, Buganda had turned against him, and Obote finally despaired of peaceful means of ruling.

When he decided to crush Buganda once and for all, Obote lit the fuse that would lead to his own destruction. Needing the support of the army, he turned to a now senior officer, Lieutenant Colonel Idi Amin. A huge, ebullient but barely literate soldier, Amin already had a reputation for brutality. Serving with the King's African Rifles in Kenya during the Mau Mau campaign, he had extracted information from his victims by threatening—and sometimes by performing—castration; and in 1962 he had narrowly escaped a murder charge for killing three Turkana tribesmen.

In Kampala, as commander of his own battalion, Amin had become friends with Obote, who in turn rewarded him with gifts that included a Mercedes limousine. When the Prime Minister married a beautiful Ganda secretary, in a lavish wedding ceremony which cost £29,000, Idi Amin was a guest of honour.

In April 1966, Amin was promoted commander of the army. One month later, on the sunlit morning of May 23, his artillery shelled the sacred palace of the Kabaka of Buganda, and Amin led his troops to storm and ransack all the buildings. Several hundred Ganda were killed, and the monarch himself, a former Cambridge student and honorary British guardsman, escaped over a wall and escaped to England, where he died in exile three years later. In Kampala, meanwhile, a grim-faced Obote abolished the constitution he had agreed with Britain and devised another, which made him Executive President with sweeping powers—but not for long.

"Harambee!"—"Let us all pull together!"—Jomo Kenyatta urged the jubilant crowds gathered in Nairobi in 1963 to celebrate Kenya's new sovereignty. With Uganda, Tanganyika and Zanzibar already independent, that gathering marked the end of years of struggle that had finally been rewarded with triumph and the attainment of independence. Four new nations had taken their place on the world stage, each of them equipped by the departing British with all the trappings of Western democracy.

The multiparty system was not, however, to take root in any of the lands. There were good reasons for its failure. Political groupings tended to be tribal in their loyalties, increasing social divisions and threatening the fragile unity of the new nation-states. Nor was there any African tradition of the loyal opposition, willing while out of power to accept with reasonably good grace the actions of its ruling rival. Unable to adapt the system to their ambitions and needs, the new nations pulled away one by one from the Westminster model until, by the end of the decade, all had become in effect one-party states.

Tanzania was the first to go. The upheavals in Zanzibar preceding the union of the two countries had had echoes on the mainland, where in early 1964 army mutineers went on the rampage, forcing President Nyerere to go into hiding. He only emerged two days later when peace had been restored by the intervention of a unit of British marine commandos dispatched at his request by Britain. This humiliating

Workers clear a site for a new village in the Tabora region of Tanzania as part of a resettlement policy launched by President Nyerere in 1967. The idea was to regroup the rural population so that it could more easily be provided with modern services.

3

experience cruelly underlined the weakness of political authority in the country, and persuaded Nyerere he should tighten his grip. By the time elections were called for the following year, he had decided—with little opposition from his fellow politicians, almost all of whom supported him—to make his TANU party the only group allowed to put up candidates. To preserve the principle of electoral choice, however, it was decided that the party should put up two nominees for each seat, leaving it up to the voters to choose between them. This system remains in force to the present day.

Nyerere was, nonetheless, aware of the possible corrupting effects of one-party rule. In 1967 he introduced a leadership code, which reflected his own idealism and was aimed to alleviate the problem. It laid down that every TANU and government leader must be either a peasant or a worker; no such politicians should henceforth hold shares in any company, or directorships in any privately owned enterprise, or receive two or more salaries, or own houses which were rented out to other people. Worried by the deepening divide between the few with privilege and money and the many without either, Nyerere called for a national drive to bridge the gap between town and village, between the élite and the majority.

The dangers he foresaw were to some extent well illustrated by the situation in neighbouring Kenya. Its new leaders had swept the nation into brash and bustling free enterprise. The sharpest pangs of land hunger were assuaged by purchasing the white estates—by 1970 half a million Africans had taken possession of two thirds of the White Highlands—but the bulk of development money was spent in Nairobi. Hotels and office blocks rose in ziggurats of concrete above the sprawling shanty towns of the periphery. Entrepreneurial ventures were fuelled by foreign investment in commerce, building construction, manufacturing, assembly plants, tourism and many other businesses. Kenya's leaders soon began to use their political positions to further private business interests, and within a few years the impoverished agitators of yesterday were flamboyantly rich. President Kenyatta became the wealthiest of them all; and his fourth wife, Mama Ngina, built her own private fortune.

Other Kenyans watched with dismay. Oginga Odinga, the leader of Kenya's Luo people, forecast trouble arising from this carnival of fortune-hunting. He warned, "A government that is isolated from the people will plunge our country into pain and tragedy." The old grievances of the colonized against their masters were being transformed into the new grievances of the many who were poor against the few who were rich. While the élite took up the settlers' pastimes of horse-racing, golf and drinks at the club, the less fortunate huddled into inadequate housing or roamed the streets looking for work. Soon a derisive name was coined for the new rich: they became known as the *Wa-Benzi*, the tribe of the Mercedes-Benz, East Africa's most prestigious and coveted car.

In 1966, Oginga Odinga broke away from KANU to form a radical opposition party, the Kenya People's Union; and in response the ageing and irascible Kenyatta banned all opposition in parliament, making Kenya a virtual one-party state. Henceforth all candidates had to be members of KANU, approved by the party's central committee. As politics and politicians lost popular support, this one-party state seemed in danger of becoming a no-party state. With the government assuming dictatorial powers, coups and counter-coups would threaten.

Similar social divisions threatened Uganda, which had its own version of the *Wa-Benzi* to contend with. Largely in response to this development, Milton Obote in 1969 launched a programme he called the Charter for the Common Man. The intention was to give ordinary Ugandans a new interest in their nation's destiny by reducing the perquisites of the political élite and levelling out regional and personal inequalities. Although less radical in its implications than the Tanzanian leadership code, the Charter had a markedly socialist tone. It emphasized reliance on Ugandan resources for the financing of development projects, rather than on borrowing abroad, and called for taxation to be used to redistribute wealth to the advantage of the minority. The Charter's details were vague, however, and it immediately caused resistance among those who feared they would lose by it. In devising and promoting the new strategy, Obote only added to his enemies at home, while alarming conservative opinion abroad, notably in Britain.

That December, a Ganda assassin shot Obote at a conference of the UPC. The bullet passed through his mouth, but did not kill him. From his hospital bed Obote ordered that Amin should be informed, and a colonel was sent over to the General's house to deliver the message. The degree of mistrust between the President and his Chief of Staff was revealingly illustrated, for when Amin learnt that soldiers were at

the door, he escaped over the back fence and fled to a loyal barracks. He plainly feared arrest; and from that moment even the pretence of loyalty between Obote and his army commander steadily dissolved. Over the next year Obote and Amin built up rival factions within the Ugandan army, and the once-disciplined force was soon dangerously divided. Its ranks had also swelled, from a thousand soldiers at the time of Independence to 9,000 by January 1971.

In that month, there was a conference of prime ministers and presidents of the countries of the British Commonwealth in Singapore, and President Obote went to join it. He flew from Entebbe airport to farewell fanfares played on ceremonial brass, expecting to be home again within the week. But that week was to stretch into long years of exile. General Amin took advantage of his absence to assume dictatorial powers. Unity by consent had failed, and unity by brute force would follow.

BRINGING IN THE COFFEE CROP

Photographs by Christopher Pillitz

Coffee is big business in East Africa. In 1958, Uganda alone produced some 210,000 tonnes of the beans, to rank sixth in the world league of producer nations. Kenya's total was 130,000 tonnes, and even Tanzania, where cultivation is less important, notched up an impressive 53,000 tonnes. Much of the crop comes from the hills, for the plant flourishes best at high altitudes in tropical climes; it thrives particularly on East Africa's rich volcanic soils.

Uganda boasts its own native plant, the *robusta* variety, which appropriately produces beans with a full, strong taste. Grown both on large estates and small farms, it is often sown alongside banana trees, which provide shade and moisture for the growing shrubs. In Kenya, however, which has no indigenous species, farmers have followed the preference of colonial planters for the more delicately flavoured *arabica*, introduced from the Arabian Peninsula at the turn of the century. Yields are lower and the strain is more difficult to grow, but the beans command a higher price on the world market, so it is preferred by plantations.

Both species have the same growing cycle. In February or March, they bear a blossom of white flowers; then a small green berry forms which turns yellow as it grows. The fruit matures to a deep red between October and December, when it is ready for picking. Within its soft flesh lies a brown husk; and this in turn contains the two seeds for which the tree is grown—the coffee beans.

Soon after dawn, a truckload of coffee pickers arrives at the Tassia Estates, north of Nairobi. To harvest the berries from the plantation's 157,000 trees, as many as 500 field workers are required each day in the high season.

Pickers move down a leafy file of coffee shrubs, removing the berries by hand. They take only the red fruit, leaving green or yellow berries to ripen further on the branch. The workers return to each tree several times during the harvest season until the whole crop has been collected.

104

Back at the sorting yard, the pickers work through piles of berries emptied from their collecting sacks to remove any stray leaves, twigs or green fruit they may have gathered accidentally. Then they load the berries into tubs which measure the quantity each worker has harvested.

Late in the afternoon, pickers carry the coffee berries up to a pulping machine, which strips the flesh from the fruit, leaving the brown husks.

With a wooden shovel, a worker turns coffee husks dumped into a tiled tank to ferment in their own juices. After anything from 12 to 36 hours, when any remaining flesh has been loosened, the husks are washed in fresh water and taken outside to dry.

At the drying racks, women smooth the wet husks into a single layer to ensure they are all exposed to the sun. After about 10 days, when the husks are dry, they will be sent to Nairobi for the final process—the extraction of the beans from their covering for sale by auction.

4

During the Kampala rush hour, shoppers and office workers weave their way through city-centre traffic. Despite the pot-holes that pit its roads, the Ugandan capital has remained a vigorous, bustling centre through two decades of coups and counter-coups.

THE MIRAGE OF PROSPERITY

After a dozen years of freedom, East Africa's presidents exercised a personal command over their nations which exceeded even the imperial fiat of the British governors they had replaced. The Western style of democracy that was envisioned at Independence, with government and opposition locked in permanent, institutionalized debate, had never taken root. But for most East Africans, respect for foreign traditions of parliamentary democracy was not the standard by which they judged their leaders. The yardstick of success or failure was rather the degree to which they had given their citizens the material benefits they had been denied under colonialism.

By this standard, East Africa's elder statesman Jomo Kenyatta was highly regarded. "The Old Man" was well into his eighties and his health was failing; he rarely appeared at the State House in Nairobi, and he was widely criticized for ruling through a clique of powerful cronies whose first priority appeared to be self-enrichment. But Kenyatta could still inspire obedience and respect. He had governed Kenya with immense skill during an era of rapid economic growth; and on February 4, 1975, the members of Kenya's National Assembly unanimously elected him to serve a third five-year term as President.

In Tanzania, Julius Nyerere also remained a popular leader. Like Kenyatta, he had been swift to stamp out serious opposition to his government; for years a number of political dissidents still languished in Tanzanian jails. But the nation's economic performance was steady if not exciting, and Nyerere's insistence on fairly sharing the benefits had inspired considerable public loyalty. While encouraging mass membership of his TANU party (renamed the Chama Cha Mapinduzi, or Revolutionary Party, in 1977), and arguing repeatedly in favour of local decision-making, Nyerere had attained such moral and intellectual ascendancy over his fellow politicians that his own views were usually accepted.

Only Uganda spoiled the picture. Although the full story of the country's devastation had yet to be revealed, it was already plain to local observers that Field Marshal Idi Amin Dada had achieved nothing in the economic area to set against the brutality of his regime. After five years in power, the burly soldier had become a tyrant on a grand scale. To oppose his wishes openly was to court violent death: rumour held that he kept the head of his most distinguished victim, the former chief justice, in a kitchen freezer. There were ominous reports of a growing bloodlust. Refugees gave horrifying accounts of government troops embarking on a campaign of genocide against the peoples of Acholi and Lango, who had supported the former President Milton Obote.

To the financiers of the West, however, it seemed on balance that East Africa was a good risk. Ugandan coffee was still fetching high prices in world markets, tempting the bankers to turn a blind eye to President Amin's excesses. In the same way Tanzania, although pledged by Nyerere to avoid excessive dependence on foreign investment, was regarded as a safe borrower; the prudence of the President's policy struck a sympathetic chord with many leaders.

Kenya was viewed with particular satisfaction. Meeting growth targets with ease, and repaying its loans promptly without apparent difficulty, the nation had become an economic milch cow which grew fatter and more productive with each injection of new capital. Gross domestic product was growing at an average annual rate of 6.6 per cent, and although the gap between rich and poor was becoming wider, almost everyone benefited to some extent from the boom.

The evidence of prosperity was especially evident throughout the capital. By the mid-1970s, Nairobi was the unrivalled commercial centre of eastern Africa, providing a base for news agencies, accountants, bankers, insurance brokers and traders of all kinds. A satellite link for telecommunications allowed business to operate as efficiently as in Europe or the U.S., while the city centre remained small and uncongested enough to cross on foot. A smart modern airport named after Kenyatta brought hundreds of thousands of tourists each year to stay at the capital's luxury hotels.

Outside Nairobi, well-maintained roads—many of them built since Independence—gave easy access to other major towns such as Nakuru in the Great Rift Valley, Kisumu on Lake Victoria and the port of Mombasa,

4

where facilities had been modernized to a high standard to handle the enormous volume of imports necessary for Nairobi's expansion. Mombasa was also a centre for the holiday trade; and one of the great tourist delights, combining the old Kenya with the new, was to travel there on the overnight train from Nairobi, with its colonial echoes in the form of mulligatawny soup for dinner and early-morning tea brought by a white-coated steward.

Objections were sometimes voiced at the "African Socialism" operating in all three countries, most notably in the growth of state bureaucracy. The old colonial marketing boards and co-operative societies had been expanded into massive government-owned corporations or "parastatals", which employed increasing numbers of people. They were expensive to run and often inefficient—partly because of poor administrative systems, lack of telecommunications and a shortage of trained personnel. But even these overstaffed corporations could be tolerated in developing economies, since the object of extending state control over commercial life was to channel all revenues through central government, which could thus determine investment policies according to national priorities.

In 1975, then, the prospects for East Africa were marred only by the clouds hovering over Uganda. But by the end of the decade, the scene had changed utterly. Kenyatta was dead, and ambitious rivals were challenging his successor, Daniel arap Moi.

Tanzania's armies had invaded and conquered Uganda, revealing a nation devastated by eight years of brutal misrule. All three countries had been thrown into economic disarray by OPEC's decision to double oil prices;

and the damage was multiplied still further when interest-rate hikes chased runaway inflation. Almost without any warning, hopes for the continuing material progress that had inspired a generation during the anti-colonial struggle faded like a mirage.

Kenyatta's death, on August 22, 1978, was a watershed in Kenya's history, and the strains and divisions in Kenyan society soon became evident to the outside world. But first there was a temporary truce, while the country united in mourning. For several days the President's body lay in state, and a long line of Africans, Asians and Europeans waited patiently in the heat before they filed past the bier. Even Oginga Odinga, the Luo leader who had been Kenyatta's bitter critic for the past decade, wept openly as he gazed for the last time on the Father of the Nation.

Resentment of the President's authoritarian style and the acquisitiveness of his family had given way to a profound sense of loss and a feeling that he had embodied a golden age. That sentiment grew when, within months of his death, interest rates soared in the wake of oil price rises, making the cost of further borrowing prohibitive. New investment slumped, Kenya's growth rate fell by half, and the balance of payments slipped into deficit. By the end of 1979, the nation's finance minister was warning Kenyans that the days of "soft options" were over.

In these worrying times, all eyes were on the new President, Daniel arap Moi, who had served as Vice-President under Kenyatta. Moi had none of his predecessor's towering authority when he succeeded to power, and sceptics doubted that this peasant's son from

Kenya's fifth largest ethnic group, the Kalenjin, could be anything more than a figurehead for the old Kikuyu establishment. He came to office with a call for Kenyans to "follow the footsteps" of leadership—and this slogan was initially taken both at home and abroad as a signal that nothing would change because of Kenyatta's death. But Moi gradually consolidated his hold over the ruling Kenya African National Union, forcing members of the old guard out of government and bringing in his own choice of men. Kenyans soon realized that the footsteps intended were not Kenyatta's but those of Moi himself, and that he intended his voice to be obeyed.

As the economic miracle began to dissolve, however, prices spiralled ahead of wages and Moi's political problems increased. A rash of sit-ins and riots at foreign-owned plantations gave the government a clear warning of the potential for widespread revolt. For the time being, however, Nairobi remained calm, and the urban workforce, forbidden by law from striking, seemed to weather the drop in living standards with stoicism. In 1981, the government was rocked by rumours linking top officials with irregular sales of maize to foreign countries, at a time when food was gravely needed at home because of a long drought.

Faced with a mounting clamour of opposition, Moi attempted to silence his critics. A number of party dissidents and university lecturers were detained without trial, and numerous academics fled into exile. But while Moi was dealing with the ideological challenge from the left, right-wing military and civilian leaders concluded that the President was too weak to run the country. At least two groups were

Blue-shirted Masai children learn to tell the time at an open-air school in a southern Kenyan village. Primary education for all children between the ages of five and 12 is an urgent priority in East Africa, where schools are funded by community groups and missions as well as by the State.

hatching plans to overthrow the government by force.

On August 1, 1982, these right-wing plotters were themselves upstaged by a group of young air force officers who led an ill-organized rebellion in Nairobi. Seizing the post office, the airport and the radio station, they gave an early-morning broadcast proclaiming their intention to "end corruption and the selling of our land to foreign interests". They were quickly joined by bus-loads of students. As news of the uprising spread, a veritable army of the poor surged into the city centre and an orgy of looting and pillaging began. Fighting raged for several hours before the rebels were crushed by regular army units, police and the élite General Service Unit. Two days later, bodies and abandoned goods still lay in the streets. The final death toll was put at 2,000 by the Church and other sources; 150 by the government.

Much of the looting and personal violence had been directed against the Asian community. Shopkeepers saw their businesses ransacked and destroyed, and the rioting spilled into secluded Asian residential areas: street after street of neat bungalows set in small gardens, where in normal times the only blacks were servants, and whites rarely penetrated. After the rebellion, many of these Asians left the country, believing that Britain or Canada would make a safer home for their children. The millionaire businessmen living in luxury suburbs like Muthaiga, where armed guards protected them from the mob, felt safe enough to stay. But many of them moved capital abroad, with damaging long-term consequences for Kenya's economy.

Moi acted swiftly in the aftermath of the coup to crush his opponents on

Bringing modern medical services to a
Masai village, a white-coated Kenyan
nurse *(below)* runs a mobile dispensary.
Emergency cases may be handled by
the European-funded flying doctor
service *(right)*, which ferries patients
from remote areas of the countryside to
city hospitals for treatment.

both left and right, and to reassure foreign investors that his government remained in control. The air force was temporarily disbanded and hundreds of its servicemen court-martialled. The University of Nairobi and Kenyatta University College were closed down for several months. And a formidable rival in the government, the Minister for Constitutional Affairs, was publicly accused of treason and forced to resign in disgrace.

With his authority once more established, Moi, like Kenyatta before him, declared his faith in capitalism and foreign investment as the route to prosperity in Kenya. The development plan for the second half of the 1980s spelt out the message: "Growth in the private sector is the core of the development process." New loans would be raised despite the cost of borrowing, and multinationals such as General Motors, Firestone, Unilever and Brooke Bond would continue to serve as "locomotives" for the economy.

In the National Assembly, some MPs questioned the value of foreign-funded development. Their argument was that such investments brought scant increase in employment and that political instability would return if Kenya's masses were not helped soon. But few disputed that industrial and commercial growth were crucial to the nation's prosperity. Agriculture could not be expanded to support a new, more populous generation, since many farms were already producing at full capacity. Irrigation schemes and land reclamation programmes could not be expected to enlarge significantly the cultivable area, totalling just 17 per cent of the land surface.

With 250,000 young people entering the job market every year, the rise in

unemployment—and the drift of population to the cities—seemed likely to continue. Despite the recession, thousands of men and women from all the rural areas still trekked to Nairobi in search of work, regardless of the "no vacancies" signs hanging from factory gates. Most of them ended up in shanty towns like Mathare Valley, on the capital's outskirts.

In these mushrooming settlements, families lived packed together in mean wooden shacks, and prostitution, theft and violence were the stuff of everyday life. Yet apart from the tiny businesses that the more fortunate of the newcomers created—running market stalls, repairing shoes, making oil lamps from tin cans—crime was the only means of survival for many of Kenya's poor.

Far from the cities, in the northern plains, pastoralists including the Turkana, the Rendille and the Somalis were experiencing a similar desperate squeeze on their resources. Drought ravaged their lands in 1981, causing the loss of thousands of cattle. Though relief agencies helped to restock herds, the process of recovery seemed likely to take years. The government, which would have preferred the pastoralists to settle, encouraged schemes to generate employment in the region—for example, by building a freezing plant for commercial fishing—but most of these projects proved to be costly failures. In fact, Catholic missions provided the pastoralists with more effective health and education facilities than the central administration.

By the mid-1980s, few Kenyans believed that the rapid growth of the Kenyatta era was likely to return. Since the abortive coup, the cloud of political instability had hovered permanently on the horizon, and national

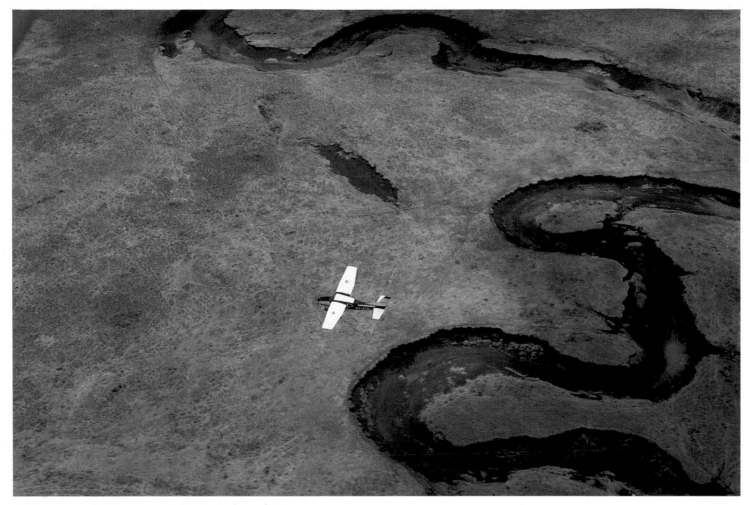

security had become the top priority for the government. Prompted by Britain and the United States, Moi had steadily increased the size of Kenya's army from the modest force he inherited from Kenyatta. So long as these forces remained loyal to the government, public discontent seemed unlikely to boil over. But if the economy were to worsen sharply, or a new conflict emerge within the ruling establishment, the danger of a second—and successful—intervention by the military could not be discounted.

Uganda's experience under Idi Amin served as an object lesson to the politicians of both Kenya and Tanzania that military rule could easily degenerate into barbarism; there was no guarantee that either peace or stability would ensue. When General Amin ousted Obote in 1971, the army was widely seen as the liberator of the nation. Many believed that his coup had been backed by Britain, in the expectation that Amin could unite Uganda and bring peace and prosperity within its grasp. Instead, the country rapidly disintegrated, and suffered the twin disasters of foreign conquest and civil war.

The economy went first. In 1972, a year after seizing power, Amin enacted his own version of the Africanization policy already carried out by Kenyatta and Nyerere. Accusing the nation's 50,000 Asians of economic sabotage, he expelled them within a month, and promised to give their property to loyal Ugandans. Asian businessmen, lawyers, engineers, administrators and doctors all joined the exodus, halting national development overnight and crippling the commercial life they had so thoroughly dominated. But African businessmen who hoped to step into the breach were soon robbed of their illusions. In a clear signal that the country would now be run by and for the army, all the Asian property was given to Amin's military henchmen.

For the next seven years, the country was systematically ransacked by the army. Generals and senior officers raided the government coffers; NCOs and privates stole from the public. Amin told his men: "Your gun is your mother and father—use it to feed yourselves." To protest or resist was to invite the most violent retribution. The military and the heavily armed police of the State Research Bureau embarked on a campaign of murder and torture. Hundreds of thousands of innocent Ugandans—including workers, peasants, politicians and priests—were seized without any warning and then killed at whim.

The most conspicuous victims were the peoples of Lango and Acholi districts, whom Amin suspected of loyalty to Obote. The former President, with 1,600 supporters, was living in Dar es Salaam as a guest of Tanzania's leader Nyerere. In 1971 he had launched an invasion which Amin had crushed without difficulty. In the aftermath, the self-appointed Field Marshal encouraged troops from his own home area, the West Nile district of northeast Uganda, to massacre potential Obote sympathizers. By 1978, whole regions of the north had lost all men of fighting age either to death or to exile.

But Amin's army was notoriously ill-disciplined, and his negligence as a commander eventually hastened his downfall. In October 1978, a mutiny by discontented troops in south-west Uganda spilt over into Tanzania's West Lake province. During a six-week-long occupation, the Ugandan soldiers deliberately destroyed farms, crops, machinery and sugar-crushing plants along the Kagera river and abducted several hundred schoolgirls before returning across the border.

This menacing intrusion persuaded Nyerere to take action. Two months

FÊTING THE NATION

On October 25 each year, Kenya celebrates its sovereignty and independence with a parade and military review in the 35,000-seat National Stadium in Nairobi. Known as Kenyatta Day, this grand occasion commemorates the arrest of Jomo Kenyatta in 1952, when Kenya's first leader was charged with organizing the Mau Mau rebellion against British rule.

Delegations travel from all over the country to march in the parade. Schoolchildren and teachers, boy scouts and girl guides, wildlife rangers and forest guards, police and prison wardens, civil servants and party members are all represented. Dancers from different regions add vigour to the spectacle and symbolize the mosaic of peoples that make up the Kenyan nation.

The climax of the event is a martial display. As jets of the Kenyan air force fly low across the stadium, detachments of the army march past in full dress uniform behind a military band. Their brilliant red tunics and red stripes on their trousers reflect the force's origins as part of the British Army and show that—like Kenyatta— independent Kenya has made peace with its former colonial rulers.

later, a disciplined Tanzanian army of some 40,000 troops, strengthened by 900 Ugandan exiles, marched north across the same border. They pressed forward almost unopposed, because Amin's army did not wish to fight for its leader. Thousands of soldiers were already fleeing north, looting shops and blowing up buildings in a frenzy of rage, before they crossed over the

borders into Sudan or Zaire. Nor was there any civilian resistance. Amin's government had produced nothing for Ugandans to take pride in or want to defend against intruders.

Late one night in April 1979, as the Tanzanian forces approached the outskirts of Kampala, whirring helicopter blades raised a dust storm among the lush flowers and shrubs of the capital's

Wearing monkey-skin hats trimmed with rosettes, trombonists lead Kenya's army band in the annual march-past at Nairobi stadium.

Nile Mansions Hotel. President Amin was escaping from the luxury suites which housed both his government and the interrogation cells where thousands of Ugandans had perished. All that night, gunfire shook the city and frightened residents cowered in their homes. But their torment was nearly over. Within days the Tanzanian army was parading through the capital and the people of Uganda came out to rejoice in the streets.

Then it was time to count the cost of eight disastrous years. Behind the shield of the advancing Tanzanian army, Ugandan journalists made their first trips for years into the north of their country. They soon discovered how badly the region had suffered. Down red-earth tracks overgrown with shoulder-high elephant grass, the reporters found village after village sunk back into isolation, far removed from any administrative support; the people were naked or dressed in rags. Everyday necessities such as soap, paraffin and farm tools were totally lacking. Hospitals and dispensaries struggled vainly to survive without supplies of drugs or medical equipment. Schools

On the palm-fringed beaches of
Kunduchi, just 15 kilometres from Dar
es Salaam, visitors can swim, skin-dive
and search for exotic shells in unspoilt
surroundings. Tanzania's tourist
industry is far less developed than
Kenya's, but provides a valuable
source of foreign currency.

had been abandoned, leaving only dim memories of former days, when Ugandans were the most highly educated of all East Africans.

In that same month of April 1979, the main factions of opposition to Amin gathered at the northern Tanzanian town of Moshi. Obote waited impatiently in Dar es Salaam, dealing through intermediaries, while an interim coalition government known as the Uganda National Liberation Front was formed. Its members, mostly exiles, pledged themselves to far-reaching reform, and promised a non-tribal democracy very different from anything in Uganda's history.

Western governments sent advisers to assess the gravity of the country's financial problems, and their findings made dismal reading. The World Bank and Commonwealth economists who flocked to Kampala estimated roughly that since 1971 the yields of coffee, the major export crop, had dropped by half. The decline in cotton, sugar and tobacco crops was even more alarming: yields had fallen to between one sixth and one eighth of the levels reached 10 years earlier. But while the government sought foreign loans and investment for much-needed imports such as farm machinery and medical supplies, these high-powered teams drew up bold and far-reaching plans for reconstruction.

More than 20,000 Tanzanian troops remained in Uganda to guarantee stability until a new Ugandan army could be formed. In the first months of peace, the horrors and fears of the Amin period were swept away by a new mood of exhilaration. Farmers and businessmen with confidence in the future seized every opportunity to rebuild their careers—and friendly outsiders were quick to give their help. A Norwegian team renovated a shattered hospital at Mbarara on the southern border, while West Germans created another pocket of normality by repairing a sophisticated salt plant at Katwe in eastern Uganda. Britain, the European Economic Community, the World Bank and the International Monetary Fund all promised loans.

The exiled Asians were urged to come back, with promises that their property would be restored. Though most preferred to wait and see how the situation developed, two of Uganda's richest Asian families, the Mehtas and the Madvanis, returned almost at once to their ruined sugar estates. Keen young men from Bombay worked tirelessly on the aged sugar-processing machinery, cannibalizing one machine to mend another and coaxing rusty parts into new life. At Lugazi, near Kampala, the Mehta family mansion was refurbished, peacocks strolled once more on the neat lawns, and at night-time the men relaxed on flood-lit tennis courts.

In those early months, few dared to contemplate the depth of Uganda's political malaise. But it soon became apparent that the years of terror and deprivation had drained the nation's will for unity. Politicians and bureaucrats seized the opportunity to enrich themselves, taking large cuts from government contracts, siphoning off funds for reconstruction raised through loans from foreign banks, and even selling food supplied by foreign charities.

More ambitious men—including Obote, who was still biding his time in Dar es Salaam—had decided that they could only rule Uganda by controlling its army, and their struggle for power

Rising behind Nairobi's colonial-style City Hall, modern office blocks and hotels testify to Kenya's post-independence boom. With the aid of heavy international investment, Nairobi has become East Africa's banking and commercial centre.

119

would soon plunge the country into civil war. General Tito Okello, an Obote loyalist who was commander of the new Uganda National Liberation Army, had begun recruiting once more in Lango and Acholi, where long lines of gaunt and ragged men rejoined the forces. In the south and west, the Ankole-born defence minister Yoweri Museveni—who was utterly opposed to Obote's return—was recruiting just as quickly amongst the Ankole and the Ganda. The two wings of the UNLF were on a collision course, and by the end of 1979 decision-making in the government was paralysed.

In Tanzania, Nyerere watched with growing anxiety as the situation deteriorated in Uganda. By mid-1980 he had become convinced that anarchy was threatening, and once again intervened to change Uganda's history. Believing that Milton Obote was the only man capable of imposing effective rule, Nyerere backed a coup against the government by a pro-Obote military council, which then called an election for December 1980.

As Nyerere and most of the other observers had expected, the victorious party turned out to be Obote's Uganda People's Congress (UPC). But the price of victory was high, for it was achieved by blatant ballot-rigging and ruthless intimidation of the opposition Democratic Party, which had overwhelming support among the Ganda people. In the course of the campaign, Democratic Party candidates and workers suffered numerous violent attacks. Even so, when Commonwealth observers arrived to monitor the last few days of polling, the Democratic Party was widely believed to be winning comfortably. But since the military council pre-empted the independent Election Commission by announcing a UPC victory hours before the official votes were expected, most Ugandans recognized that a massive electoral fraud had taken place. Once again, democracy had collapsed.

The subsequent conduct of the new government bore out Museveni's worst fears. Obote rejected all possibility of reconciliation between the north and south, and showed little zeal for eliminating corruption. Despite optimistic predictions of economic recovery by World Bank and IMF observers, and improved harvests on coffee and tea estates, living standards continued to deteriorate for most Ugandans.

Worse still, the soldiers recruited by Okello took up rapine and murder like Amin's troops before them. The terrorizing of rural communities to extract food was tacitly sanctioned by Obote's government, and human rights organizations in the United States and Britain estimated that 100,000 people, most of them defenceless peasants, were killed by marauding soldiers between 1980 and 1985.

But in the dense bush around Luwero to the north of Kampala—part of the former kingdom of Buganda—Yoweri Museveni was busy organizing his own guerrilla force, the National Resistance Army (NRA). Ganda and, later, Ankole peasants left their villages to swell the ranks. And when written programmes underlined the movement's commitment to full democracy and a strong, independent economy, many educated youths fled Kampala to join the guerrillas.

By the middle of 1985 Museveni's men controlled large tracts of southern Uganda, depriving the government of revenues from the richest coffee-growing estates. The guerrillas also

Children scamper past wood and tin shacks in Nairobi's oldest and largest shanty town, in the Mathare river valley. The slum grew rapidly as rural migrants, joined by refugees from Somalia and Ethiopia, pushed the city's population from under 120,000 in 1948 to over a million in 1985.

4

Two Asian women dressed in saris stroll along one of Nairobi's main shopping streets. Many of the stores are owned by Kenyan Asians, who maintain a powerful presence in the commercial and financial sectors of the economy despite government policies to promote more African involvement.

had severe supply problems, but their successes had been sufficient to scare the army. Convinced that Obote was losing his grip, General Okello and his army of northerners made a sudden dash south early in July and seized the capital. A convoy of Mercedes cars drove Obote and his closest followers across the Kenyan border on their way to a second exile in Zambia.

The new military regime promised to restore unity to Uganda and entered peace talks with the NRA in Nairobi. But a truce signed at Christmas 1985 was ignored by both sides; and they continued to prepare for a fight to the finish. In an alarming development for Museveni, Okello decided to welcome back troops from Amin's old army, who had been sheltering in Sudan and Zaire, and rearmed them to join the onslaught against the NRA.

But the momentum of the southern forces was not to be denied. In January 1986 the NRA encircled, then captured, Kampala. As Okello fled north, the former defence minister was sworn in as the eighth president of independent Uganda, wearing a private's uniform to symbolize his concern for the ordinary people of the nation. In another well-publicized gesture, he had the luxury beds removed from the presidential suite, and installed a simple couch made by a local carpenter.

The change of mood from pessimism to optimism was palpable; and when the NRA managed to drive the northern armies back aross the Nile, taking over their strongholds one by one with little loss of life, hope rapidly spread throughout the nation that stability might finally be in sight. Even the northern people had tired of war. In the words of one Lango elder: "If you are reading a book, it is necessary to turn the page. The people want a new spirit, and they want peace."

Three months before Museveni took power in Uganda, Julius Nyerere stepped down as President of Tanzania. He had kept his country united through the expensive conquest and occupation of Uganda; he had steered it through the hazards of a devastating economic crisis. And in October 1985, he had become the first of East Africa's leaders to hand over power voluntarily to his successor. It was a remarkable demonstration of his commitment to the constitutional process. At the age of 63, Nyerere was still massively popular with his countrymen, admired especially for his personal integrity. It was well known that he had amassed no private fortune; at his small farm in northern Tanzania, Nyerere owned just six cows and a vegetable garden.

Yet the political inheritance Nyerere passed on to his successor, Ali Hassan Mwinyi, was written off as worthless by many critics. The stability he had nurtured could not be disputed; nor could the social benefits such as improved health and education, which had consistently been given preference over both commercial and industrial growth. But Tanzania's economic performance had been a disappointment. Even the once elegant and thriving city of Dar es Salaam was crumbling and ill-maintained.

From the earliest days of Independence, Nyerere had insisted on the nation's self-reliance, both in politics and economics. To foster this spirit he had demanded a decisive break with the colonial past, regardless of the cost, and the choice of a socialist economic policy was part of this strategy. In Nyerere's words, independent Tanzania was casting off "the capitalist attitude of mind" which colonialism brought into Africa. By emphasizing national effort, not foreign investment, as the major instrument of development, Nyerere hoped that his country would pull itself up to prosperity by its own bootstraps.

Outside help remained essential, however, for all Nyerere's aspirations. Tanzania sought aid from China and Scandinavia—countries that were new to East Africa, but shared similar characteristics of large land surfaces and scattered populations. In 1970, blue-uniformed Chinese labourers started to work on the massively ambitious Uhuru railway, from Lusaka in Zambia to the port of Dar es Salaam, which would open a new trade route through the south of Tanzania. More than 1,000 kilometres of track were laid in the next five years. The immense cost was paid for by Chinese loans, which were later rescheduled so generously that they were effectively written off. Meanwhile, Scandinavian economists, sociologists and agriculturists disappeared into Tanzania's remote and impoverished villages to hasten the farming revolution.

The basic strategy in agriculture was outlined in the Arusha Declaration. Nyerere delivered it in February 1967 in a town of the same name in the pastoral highlands of the north. Promoting the ideal of *ujaama*—meaning neighbourliness, or community action—he announced that families living in scattered hamlets and homesteads were to be brought together in villages, so that basic services such as roads, water supplies, schools and dispensaries could reach them more effectively. Each family would put in labour on communal fields, while maintaining

An old settler farmhouse, set amongst spreading lawns on the slopes of Mount Kenya, recalls the days when the White Highlands—a 650-square-kilometre swathe of land north of Nairobi—were restricted to European ownership. By the mid-1980s, most of the land had been sold to Africans.

an individual plot for food crops. The villages were to organize co-operative trading ventures to market their cash crops and import such basic necessities as fertilizer, tools and seeds.

The early years of the scheme were an utter failure. There was no trained body of political cadres to organize the villages, so the policy was often poorly understood, badly implemented and frequently resisted by the peasants themselves. There was not enough foreign currency available to purchase the new equipment needed, nor enough lorries, spare parts, fuel or even roads to carry what was available to the villages.

By 1973, the planners concluded that fewer but bigger villages were necessary, and so the policy moved into a dramatic second phase. During the "Operation Tanzania", which was completed in 1977, about 13 million people moved into new settlements, so that 85 per cent of rural Tanzanians were gathered into just 7,300 villages with an average population of almost 2,000 each. There was little consultation with the peasants themselves and considerable compulsion was used to move them, particularly at the beginning of the exercise.

Despite the hardships of these early years, most Tanzanians gained some benefits from the relocation. Basic facilities were supplied throughout the country, bringing roads and services to regions that had been isolated for centuries. By 1985, the provision of clean water, medical centres and schools was considered by a United Nations body to be the best in Africa. But in terms of self-reliance, the results were frustrating. The rise in the cost of imports following the global inflation of the 1970s meant that village co-operatives could

not afford the fertilizers and tractors essential to their success. And without these advantages, the new villagers—who had no tradition of collective organization—were not easily persuaded to work together to increase their export crop production.

Since agriculture produces 80 per cent of the nation's export earnings, and provides 85 per cent of all employment, the effect on the national economy was devastating. Between 1975 and 1982, the volume of agricultural exports actually fell by a third, and Tanzania was obliged to spend 20 per cent of its import budget on cereals in order to feed both urban and rural communities. The crisis triggered off some rethinking of policies. With only one third of the potential farming land under cultivation in 1985, improvement remained a possibility, but it was clear that Tanzania's problems would

grow increasingly grave if production did not recover soon.

The small industrial sector, producing basic items such as processed foods, prepared timber, leather, textiles, batteries and tyres, as well as assembling cars and trucks, suffered from a shortage of expertise and capital. At Independence, most of these businesses were in white or Asian hands; in 1967, however, the majority were nationalized, and expatriates and Asian Tanzanians began to leave. The slow drain of Asian capital accelerated in the early 1980s, when many of the remaining Asian businesses were raided by the police because they were trading on the black market during a time of shortage. By the mid-1980s, industry was operating at only 40 per cent of total capacity.

Shortage of foreign currency also hampered Tanzania's development in

Deposits of soda ash turn the dry bed of Lake Magadi into a patchwork of browns and greys *(below)*. The mineral reserves, constantly renewed by saline springs, are piped to a plant on the shore *(opposite page)* for processing, then sold for use in the paper, glass and fertilizer industries.

the 1970s and the early 1980s. On principle Nyerere had rejected external investment in Tanzanian businesses, but he was obliged to raise funds abroad for major public projects. With great diplomatic finesse, he persuaded the United States to build a tarmac road to Zambia alongside the Chinese railway, and to assist such agricultural schemes as seed improvement and tsetse fly control. More than a dozen other gov-

ernments provided Tanzania with similar grants.

At the same time Tanzania was also borrowing steadily from overseas banks; by 1975 its debt totalled $750 million. In that period interest and capital repayments amounted to only 5 per cent of export earnings, which seemed unlikely to threaten the independence and self-reliance on which Nyerere placed such stress. By 1980,

however, a jump in interest rates, combined with higher import prices and lower earnings from farm crops, had left Tanzania desperately short of foreign currency, and dependent on raising new loans not only to fund the development budget, but simply to balance the current account.

The IMF offered some respite with a $235 million loan over two years. Stringent conditions were attached to

Outside Zanzibar town, two children spread out piles of cloves to dry in the sun. The clove plant—shown on the left in a 19th-century drawing—is the cash crop on which the island's economy principally depends. Its buds, which must be hand-picked, are desiccated then sold as a spice.

the loan, however—devaluation of the Tanzanian shilling by as much as 40 per cent, mass lay-offs throughout the civil service, privatization of industry and services, and relaxation of import controls for Tanzanians holding capital abroad. Nyerere feared that such policies would cause high unemployment, especially in the towns, and a sudden rise in food prices. Arguing that many Tanzanians were already living at the lowest possible level, Nyerere predicted that some would die of starvation if the measures were put into effect. He refused to implement the conditions and the deal collapsed.

An additional reason for Nyerere's reluctance to accept the IMF deal was undoubtedly the fact that it would have meant dismantling much of the edifice of Tanzania's socialist system and decimating the country's bureaucracy. The political consequences of such an act would have been considerable, because the machine was staffed almost exclusively with supporters of his ruling CCM party. Yet ironically the bureaucracy had been a target for many of his own fiercest criticisms. He had blamed officials for incompetence and arrogance, declaring that "There is a tendency for all levels of government to act as if the peasants were of no account". Others would add the charge of corruption. As Tanzania's economy went into decline and times grew harder, bribery had become widespread and, in 1981, ministry and corporation officials were implicated in a million-dollar scandal over the illegal renting of government cars.

Yet despite Tanzania's problems, her political stability was only threatened twice during Nyerere's tenure of office. In 1983 a plot was uncovered amongst a disaffected faction within the army, but the leaders were quickly arrested. Their trial was conducted with little sense of urgency, and although eight officers were eventually sentenced to life imprisonment, the evidence uncovered indicated that the conspiracy had never had the slightest chance of success.

A deeper challenge to long-term stability came from the Zanzibaris, whose close traditional links with the Gulf States had given rise to a more capitalistic ethic and commercial spirit. Their own economy, based on sugar and cloves, had nose-dived even more dramatically than the mainland's, provoking some Zanzibaris to campaign for independence. But an attempt to end Zanzibar's union with the mainland was headed off at the CCM party congress in 1984. Diplomatically, the man chosen by the party to stand for election to the Tanzanian presidency to replace Nyerere was the President of Zanzibar, Ali Mwinyi.

Since the electoral system allows only one candidate, selected by the National Executive Committee, to be presented for approval or disapproval, Mwinyi's confirmation by the electorate was perhaps a foregone conclusion. However, with 90 per cent of the voters registering approval, a smooth transfer of power was guaranteed. Nyerere remained as part-time party chairman, suggesting that Tanzania's leaders would continue to emphasize national self-reliance over economic growth for the rest of the 1980s.

With new leaders established in all three nations by 1986, East Africa faced the challenges of the future with some grounds for optimism. Peace in Uganda promised to provide a welcome economic fillip for both its neighbours; and stable government could allay fears that war might again spill over the borders. If the three nations would co-operate economically, observers pointed out, they might find means of developing their own resources without increasing the burden of foreign debt. But relations between the countries remained distressingly tense. Despite Museveni's efforts to construct diplomatic bridges, the left-leaning President was regarded with suspicion by Moi and Ali Mwinyi.

Distrust of each other's motives had dogged the three East African nations since the first days of Independence. Paradoxically, co-operation had been greater under the British, when tax, customs and excise, post and telecommunications, and railways and airlines serving East Africa had been administered jointly. All attempts to sustain and strengthen such links after the lands gained sovereignty had only ended in failure.

An ambitious effort had been made in 1967, when the three governments signed a Treaty of East African Co-operation. By the terms of this agreement, free trade was encouraged and scarce resources pooled, in order to reduce the costs of development and avoid wasteful competition in basic industries. A supranational institution called the East African Community was established in luxurious new offices at Arusha, to administer the common services. At the same time, an East African Development Board was set up to channel the bulk of new investment to Tanzania and Uganda, so that their infrastructure was brought up to Kenyan standards.

The Community had some success in export markets, and signed a promising trade agreement with the EEC. But problems began when Amin seized power in Uganda. Nyerere's refusal to recognize the new regime and his encouragement of Obote's failed invasion attempt of 1971 enraged Amin, who retaliated by closing Uganda's border with Tanzania and effectively withdrawing from the Community.

Relations between Tanzania and Kenya were also deteriorating. The balance of trade between the two countries was greatly in Kenya's favour. In addition, there was personal friction between Nyerere and the Kenyan leader Jomo Kenyatta, which drifted into mutual contempt. In 1974, Tanzania temporarily closed its border with Kenya, claiming that heavy trucks from the north were damaging its roads. When, three years later, Kenyatta seized control of the jointly owned East African Airways, which had fallen heavily into debt to Kenyan banks, the border was closed yet again and the Community was dead.

After Kenyatta's death and his replacement by Moi, relations improved a little. When Obote returned to power in Uganda in 1980, the three governments were finally able to negotiate a share-out of the residual property of the East African Community. Though the borders were opened once again, free trade was not restored.

The collapse of the East African Community weakened all three countries at a time of grave economic crisis. Between 1980 and 1985 the market prices for coffee, tea and sugar dropped alarmingly by comparison with the boom years of the 1960s. East Africa's reliance on a narrow range of crops was cruelly underlined by a simultaneous fall in cotton and sisal prices, accelerated by competition from synthetic materials. While export earnings shrunk, the cost of essential imports mushroomed. Oil and oil-based fertilizers, trucks, buses, farm machinery and tractors, medicines and surgical equipment, printing materials and books: they all became more expensive, and were consequently in short supply throughout the region.

The effect on Kenya and Tanzania was to halt development virtually in its tracks. Uganda suffered even more, because of the destruction of war. Schools without books and hospitals without drugs were commonplace in all three countries. Especially in the countryside, roads fell into disrepair, while vehicles lay unused for lack of fuel or spare parts. Shortages of fertilizer and farm machinery brought harvests down from the high yields of the 1960s. A cycle of decline set in that only seemed likely to be broken if interest rates fell enough to revive the world

4

In Tanzania, rows of sisal plants
stretch towards the horizon. Sisal fibre,
used for rope-making, is a major
export crop, amounting in boom years
to one third of world output. Yet the
entire national stock was propagated
from only 62 plants illegally imported
from Latin America in 1892.

economy and reduce the heavy burden of East Africa's debt.

The collapse into economic stagnation might have been alleviated had the East African nations been able to generate more regional trade. But their mutual antagonisms prevented this. Instead, the scant amount of cash was translated into poverty, hunger and a threat of widespread starvation. Bad harvests sharpened the emergency, especially in Kenya and Tanzania, where drought in the early 1980s hastened the decline of farm yields.

The problem of inadequate food supplies was compounded by the fact that the birth rates were soaring. No figures were available for Uganda, but in Kenya and Tanzania, where reliable census material was at hand, it was estimated that in 1986 there were twice as many people to feed as at Independence, and the figure was expected to double again by the turn of the century. Despite a $20 million family planning campaign, Kenya's rate of population growth, at 4 per cent a year, was the highest in the world, and Tanzania followed close behind, at around 3.5 per cent.

To keep their economies afloat, Kenya and Uganda were both forced to borrow from the IMF on similar terms to those Tanzania's President Nyerere had turned down. As a condition of lending, the Fund demanded that each country devalue its currency, reduce the numbers employed by the parastatal agencies, increase payments to local farmers and cut down on food subsidies for town-dwellers.

East Africa's leaders were aware of the danger that such measures were bound to increase the poverty of their citizens, and perhaps even spark off revolution. But only Nyerere was prepared to campaign for a common front in negotiating with the foreign bankers. Shortly before bowing out from Tanzania's presidency, he addressed the problem in a speech to an audience of bankers and businessmen at London's Guildhall. He put the case for a new international economic order which would give the countries fair prices for the agricultural produce they sent abroad, so that they could once again buy the necessary imports— lacking for a decade or more—and continue building up the social infrastructure of housing, roads, hospitals and schools. Otherwise, he warned, East Africa would never be able to repay its debts and the risk of political upheaval would continue to grow.

In 1986, however, economic conditions suddenly improved. When Brazil's coffee crop failed because of frost, international coffee prices doubled, guaranteeing healthy profits for Kenya and Uganda. There were also signs that world interest rates might ease. And a change of policy at the World Bank suggested that loan agencies might take a more sympathetic view of the problems faced by East African countries.

These welcome developments did not presage a quick solution to the region's problems, nor did they smooth the way for co-operation among the neighbours. However, they provided the region's leaders with some room to manoeuvre. "When elephants fight," goes a traditional saying, "the grass gets trampled"; and with peace restored at last, recovery could begin. By devoting more resources to food production, to alleviate the hunger of their citizens, the politicians could pave the way to a more solid phase of nation-building in the future.

In a village near Kampala, a woman sits outside her home weaving a basket from dried grass. In common with much of contemporary East African life, the scene blends old and new: basket-weaving is an ancient craft, but the house is modern and the woman wears cotton instead of barkcloth.

THE VILLAGE AND THE CITY

At dawn the flamingoes rise in a flurry of pink to pierce the pearl-grey mists above Lake Baringo, in the Great Rift Valley of Kenya. The sky clears quickly with the warmth of morning, the humps of hippopotamuses appear like tiny islands in the middle distance, and fish eagles cruise high above the lake, scanning its deep blue waters for their prey. On the surrounding wooded hillsides, patches of mist still linger amidst branches of thorn and acacia, and mingle with the smoke of early morning cooking fires.

To the visitor, this beautiful landscape looks serene and unchanging. But to the Pokot, a community of over 100,000 people whose homesteads dot the hillsides around, change is at their doorstep: because this is frontier territory, a borderland between two different worlds. To the north, the Great Rift Valley opens into an ancient land, a vast arid wilderness stretching past Lake Turkana to the borders of Sudan and Ethiopia. Few roads pass that way, and there is scarcely a trace of modern civilization apart from a few mission centres and government posts, and the occasional store selling pots, knives and cloth.

To the south of Pokot territory lies the new world. The towns of Kitale, Eldoret and Kericho have sprung up in Kenya's most fertile soils, among large estates where tea and coffee crops are grown. Main roads and the railway pass through the Great Rift Valley, carrying all the paraphernalia of urban society to the Kipsigis, Nandi and Tugen peoples, who, like the Pokot, belong to a larger group known as the Kalenjin. These southern peoples now use tractors to plough their lands, and they sell their produce through state marketing boards; their children go to school and learn English; and one famous Kalenjin, Daniel arap Moi, has become the President of Kenya.

Between these two worlds, aware of both yet belonging fully to neither, the Pokot preserve a cautious balance. Many have long been farmers; others have taken to cultivation only since the drought of 1981, when thousands of their cattle died of starvation. Many more still hold to the pastoral life; they raise cattle for their milk and goats for their flesh, and grow only a couple of crops necessary for survival. But almost all Pokot resist the advance of modernity, seeing no reason to change what suits them well.

Lokiorongolol, a rich Pokot herdsman about 50 years old, lives close to Lake Baringo with his five wives, their children and a few relatives; their homestead consists of five or six low thatched buildings surrounded by a thorn stockade, which also encloses byres for the cattle. The needs of these two or three dozen sleek, long-horned beasts set the daily pattern of family life. At sunrise the children milk the cows and collect dung to dry for the fires, while the women heat a stew of

5

On the shores of Lake Victoria, Luo fishermen repair their nets beside beached sailing canoes. The lake supplies three quarters of the freshwater fish landed in Kenya; the bulk of catches is Nile perch, which was introduced in colonial times.

goat's meat and dried berries. By the time Lokiorongolol appears, the sun is climbing above the tallest trees, and the younger men and boys are leading the cattle out to pasture, urging them on with cries and whistles.

Lokiorongolol, lean and lined, remains at the homestead, watching his senior wife Cheponcigil and her four co-wives as they fetch water and firewood, repair the huts and byres, tan leather for clothes, or tend their vege-table gardens. He offers comments now and then, but generally leaves the women to do as they think best. The slow, familiar routine keeps them and their little girls busy—though with plenty of time for talk—until the cattle come home at dusk. The animals are tethered in their byres and milked again; and then the second meal of the day begins. In the evening, the family sit around the embers of the fire, talking amongst themselves or with visi-tors from neighbouring homesteads, until it is time to sleep.

As the elder of the homestead, Lokiorongolol is a pillar of the social order. He settles arguments in the homestead patiently and with care, seldom having to raise his voice to exercise the authority he is acknowledged to possess. And he guides the family's dealings with other Pokot families, negotiating the number of cattle to be given as bridewealth, for ex-

132

ample, when one of his sons marries.

Like all Pokot elders, Lokiorongolol also helps to arrange the cycle of ceremonies, or rites of passage, through which his people pass from childhood to old age. Boys are circumcised at the age of about 15, and then initiated as young warriors; later in life, when they are married and have their own homesteads and children, they in turn will become elders. Girls must submit to the acute pain of female circumcision, as a prelude to marriage. When they are beyond child-bearing, they reach a new status as respected matrons.

Even today, the Pokot barely admit the existence of modern Kenya. They are fully aware of the goods on sale, yet they buy nothing from the towns save beads to weave into necklaces, or iron tools and spearheads. Though they guard their cattle as carefully as city investors watch the stock market, they do not breed these pampered beasts for trading or speculation; the Pokot treasure their cattle as symbols of wealth, securities which they exchange for wives, but will only kill on ceremonial occasions. They sell cattle only in the direst emergencies.

Yet the Pokot are not ignorant of the new world. They make a conscious effort to keep in touch, and with every generation they send one or two of their brightest children to school, to learn the modern ways and acquire the latest knowledge. Such emissaries act as informed mediators when the woodland homesteads are visited by authority: tax collectors, game wardens, policemen looking for criminals in flight, or a whole range of people who come in cars to advise the Pokot how to live differently and, say these advisers, live better. Lokiorongolol and his fellow elders receive these various missions

With a catch of Nile perch lashed to his bicycle, a Luo fishmonger pedals back to his village, 25 kilometres from Lake Victoria. More distant communities make do with dried fish, though refrigerated stocks are sent by rail to Nairobi and other inland towns.

according to their status, and listen to what they have to say. But they go on living as before. The world of drains and hygiene, machines and motor transport simply has no appeal.

Few other groups in East Africa have preserved traditions so resolutely. Some pastoralists, like the Karamojong of Uganda, the Masai of Tanzania, the Turkana and Somali of Kenya, have also remained for the most part loyal to their old ways of life. But most communities have adapted willingly to the new world. Some, whose lands are favoured by rainfall and high fertility, grow crops for cash and spend their money on fertilizers and pesticides, sandals and machine-made clothes, radios and bicycles. Others, in regions beset by drought, war or land shortage, have abandoned the countryside and sought a better future in the cities. They have lost much in the process, cutting themselves off from family and friends, cherished customs and long-held beliefs. But for the luckiest and most enterprising among them, the rewards have been outstanding.

A prosperous medical practitioner in Nairobi, known to his friends as Dr. Paul, has no doubts that life has changed for the better since his childhood in a small Kikuyu village. His wife runs a successful hairdressing salon; two of his four children are at university in England, and the other two are studying at the best boarding school in Kenya. Outside the family house in Muthaiga, the capital's most exclusive suburb, stands a gleaming Mercedes which the doctor drives himself, a Toyota for his wife, and an estate car for family trips through the Kenyan countryside.

Now aged 50, Paul was just 13 years old when the first rumblings of the Mau Mau rebellion reached his village. Relatives advised him to leave home and seek education in Uganda, well known at the time for the quality of its schools. He set off with no more than the name of a school, some 300 kilometres away, where he had no friends or relatives to support him. Paul occasionally managed to cadge lifts from passing lorries; once or twice he rode pillion on bicycles. The rest of the way he walked: it took him a week.

The school, when he found it, was a miserable, run-down establishment.

5

The straw-thatched roof leaked when it rained and smelled like rotting fruit in the sun. But Paul was in luck. The Ganda headmaster, who owned the school, was willing to take anyone who came, and although there were scarcely any books he and his two teachers managed to instil a thirst for knowledge into the hundred or more pupils.

Paul became the headmaster's servant to pay his keep, and was given a bed in an outhouse. He would wake up before it was light to go to the well for water, take the goats out to pasture, then weed the vegetable patch or dig some new ground. In the evenings he worked again, digging or weeding. For breakfast he had a cup of milkless tea and a piece of yam, plantain or manioc, cooked by the headmaster's wife, and supper was equally simple.

It was a tough apprenticeship, but Paul stuck to his purpose. After three years, the headmaster sent him to a bigger secondary school in Toro, 200 kilometres further away from the land of his birth. Paul spent five years here and then won a scholarship to study medicine at the University of East Africa at Makerere, just outside Kampala, which attracted the top students from the whole region. By now Paul could speak both the Toro and the Ganda languages as well as English, Swahili and his own Kikuyu. As he progressed towards his doctorate in the cosmopolitan atmosphere of Makerere, he forged friendships with many students from distant parts and different backgrounds. When they met later in Nairobi or Dar es Salaam, or even overseas, these rising stars of the new African meritocracy would talk of their days at the campus, or their nights in Suzanna's Club or the White Nile—two famous dance halls of Kampala—

drinking beer and dancing with bar girls and nurses to live bands playing the fashionable Congolese jazz.

Kenyatta was released from prison the year Paul qualified, and when Independence came the young doctor was a City Medical Officer in Nairobi. By this time he was married to a girl from his own Kikuyu district. They moved into a flat in a rough part of town; these were days when scarcely any blacks could afford to live in the best residential areas. After a few years, though, he opened a private practice which soon attracted many wealthy clients; and eventually Paul himself grew rich enough to buy a six-bedroomed house with wide lawns and a swimming pool. Now its electrically operated gates are guarded 24 hours a day by a security man, and Dr. Paul's three servants live in a small outbuilding behind the garage—a cook, a gardener and a houseboy, who doubles as butler and general factotum.

Dr. Paul still gives one evening's consultation a week at the public hospital—working alongside harassed and poorly paid colleagues who have no private patients—but for the most part the rigours of poverty are behind him. One afternoon a week he drives to the Limuru Club for a round of golf. Here, in the elegant surroundings once reserved for top colonial officials, he can relax with other members of Kenya's élite—ministers, permanent secretaries, businessmen and lawyers—and with professionals from abroad. Like them, he has become a member of a community which is far more international than truly African.

The population of Nairobi has more than trebled since Dr. Paul arrived in 1962; by the mid-1980s it was growing

at the alarming pace of 8 per cent a year, double the national rate. For late and less fortunate arrivals facing the hazards of economic recession, the prospects of finding work, let alone climbing the ladder to success, are extremely bleak. Yet thousands of peasants leave the countryside each year. Similar tides of immigration have engulfed Kampala and Dar es Salaam.

The new arrivals to the cities may be driven by hunger, by curiosity or by ambition, and they are united by a common urge to better themselves quickly. In the countryside, they may face years of hard work to achieve the most modest success; the city offers the promise—in practice, however, rarely realized—of instant prosperity for themselves and for the families they leave behind. And with more than half the population of East Africa aged less than 20, optimism about the future is in good supply.

During the boom years of the 1960s, young men and women with only a few years of education could prosper. New opportunities were constantly available for clerks, office boys, policemen, nurses, teachers and engineering assistants; and with many of the jobs came a two-room flat on a housing estate, or a room in the lines of unadorned but functional blocks of flats built for employees of the public services. There was a sense of urgency and glamour about it all, and since a good job meant higher status for the whole family, parents in rural areas sent their children off with pride.

This first generation of townspeople had been brought up with traditional expectations. Most of them went to the cities planning to work for a few years until they had enough money to buy their own farm in the countryside and

Thatched homesteads—one ringed by a fence—nestle side by side in the hills of south-west Uganda. Each family grows maize, sweet potatoes, beans, peas and sorghum in its fields. The crops are stored in the small round huts, built on stilts for ventilation.

cattle to pay bridewealth, get married and bring up a family. "What is misery for the men of this world?" asked a Kenyan pop song of the 1960s. "It's a man without land, a man without a child, a man without wealth. What is misery for the woman of this world? It's a woman without a husband, without a mother, without a brother."

The bonds of family and rural living remained strong for the new migrants, and they still felt the traditional obligation to help friends and relatives when luck came their way. They would share their homes with later arrivals and feed them while they looked for work. And in the alien environment of the city, much wider tribal bonds be-

came important. Those who had travelled farthest, and could not make regular trips back to their villages, prepared to lodge near people from their home region, even if they had never met before, and so formed tribal villages in the cheaper parts of town.

In some ways, the tribe proved more important in the town than in the countryside. Men who were slow to learn Swahili, the dominant language in Nairobi and Dar es Salaam, or Ganda in Kampala, tended to stay in the tribal enclaves and not mix with other groups. And although intermarriage between different ethnic groups was common in the towns, many migrants who decided to live permanently in the

cities brought wives from their home district, because of an imbalance between the sexes. In 1969, a population survey showed that there were 153 men for every 100 women in Nairobi, 146 men for every 100 women in Kampala, and 131 men for every 100 women in Dar es Salaam.

Church and mosque went some way in helping to break down the tribal differences. Perhaps 10 per cent of East Africans today profess the Islamic faith, and about 40 per cent are Christian. Far from the family shrine, thousands of townspeople who had first been versed in the Bible or the Koran at a small village school made new friends among fellow-believers to

whom by birth and blood they were not even remotely related.

In addition to their Catholic and Protestant communities, East African cities have also witnessed a remarkable flowering of independent Christian churches, formed almost entirely by charismatic preachers who have split away from the missions. They offer a form of Christianity geared towards traditional African life. They often accept polygamous marriages, and in many cases hold circumcision cere-

monies for both boys and girls in their teens. Rejecting Western culture, they avoid the prosperous city centres: the Church of Christ in Africa, one of the largest independent churches, built its cathedral on the outskirts of Nairobi, and draws most of its congregation from among the poor. In such parts of the cities, where modern health and education facilities are almost non-existent, the CCA and other independent churches provide traditional education and health care—curing with

ancient medicines of bark and herbs.

Diviners offer a rival service, calling on the spirits of traditional religion to help their clients gain advancement, solve problems or seek revenge. Such figures have always been common in the countryside. As recently as 1960, a famous Tanzanian diviner claimed to command rampaging lions and sold magic sticks with which to fend them off. Now, the men and women who diagnose problems—probably by casting coffee beans or shells to form a pattern—and then offer to cure them with the aid of folk medicines or spells are active in most East African towns as well. According to one estimate there were 700 diviners operating in Dar es Salaam in 1967, giving a total of 10,000 consultations daily not only to the poor, but to office workers, businessmen and even senior politicians.

Despite the vigour with which such traditional beliefs have survived in the towns, the intense conditions and high pressure of urban living have taken a heavy toll. As villagers become townspeople and bring up families who have never experienced the quiet rhythms of the countryside, a new African is being formed, whose behaviour is no longer guided by custom, and whose mental outlook is shaped less by tradition than by an urban lifestyle recognizable anywhere in the world, from Bombay to Rio, from Manila to New York.

Old ways have been disappearing fast. Western-style marriages, complete with a white dress for the bride and wedding-cake receptions, have replaced the days of feasting common at rural weddings, and bridewealth is now often paid in cash, not in cattle. Traditional gifts of bales of cloth, or vats of maize beer, are increasingly replaced by smaller presents: a piece of woven cloth or a bottle of expensive imported wine, for example. Funerals, which once called for a gathering of relatives from miles around, perhaps with a sacrifice and days of feasting, may now be marked only by a graveside ceremony and a party.

Housing conditions have accelerated the change. Cramped inside four walls, the new African has far less space to fulfil the social obligations honoured for generations in the villages. Rural homesteads had a patch of open ground and several small houses, so that relatives could visit for weeks at a time, but urban families packed into small flats are hard pressed to give the expected welcome to visitors from the country. Since they cannot grow their own crops, they may not be able to afford to feed guests as liberally as custom demands. And the days when wage earners would struggle to support a new arrival from the village for several months while he looked for a suitable job have long since passed.

By the 1970s, the infrastructure of most East African cities had collapsed under the high tide of migration. The building programmes had been woefully inadequate, and new housing estates, transport facilities, hospitals and schools were soon overwhelmed by the rush. The economic slowdown in Kenya and Tanzania cut back the availability of jobs almost as drastically as the disruption of the Amin years in Uganda. The required standards of education rose even higher, driven up by the pressure of supply and demand, until several years of schooling were the expected minimum even of doormen and office sweepers.

With jobs and homes at such a premium, the townspeople became even more desperately inventive. To make enough money to get by, a man who could drive might repair a decrepit car with scrap metal and wire, and set up as a taxi driver. Another would become a middleman, an agent whose main asset was knowledge of who needed what and who could supply it. Women might set up in the market with scraps of food begged, borrowed or stolen, while others made flashy dresses out of cheap cloth and walked the streets or hovered in bars. In all the big cities, the most ruthless of all became robbers, operating in gangs armed with machetes or even pistols: the fear of violent crime became the abiding nightmare of the wealthy.

The homeless seized whatever space was available and built shanty towns from whatever materials were lying around. If the land was close to the town centre, there was probably something wrong with it: perhaps a road was planned, or the ground flooded in the rainy season, or sewers disgorged there. But those with nowhere else to stay put up their shacks overnight, worrying about the disasters only when they struck.

The authorities in all three countries at first tried to ignore these eyesores, and hoped that they would disappear in a matter of months. Instead, they not only survived but they have grown, cancer-like, forming whole neighbourhoods in which perhaps a quarter of the urban population resides. Even now there is a reluctance to acknowledge them formally, or to supply them with running water or electricity; the largest shanty town in Nairobi lay unconnected to the city water mains for several years before it was accepted as permanent, and finally connected.

Musa, who works as a messenger, lives in just such a shanty town in Kampala. He shares a tiny shack with hammered tin walls with his wife, four children, a niece and a nephew. Inside, the hovel is divided by a stretch of hessian cloth to form one room for Musa and his wife, another for the children. They cook outside on an open fire between three stones, and use a covered pit for a latrine.

The family arrived in 1984 from a village 40 kilometres from the capital. Musa's parents' plot was too small to support them, and because he had

No small town in East Africa is complete without a bar, sometimes doubling as a general store. A landmark in the community, its presence—and its wares—are often advertised by vivid decorations painted by enthusiastic local artists. Although soft drinks like Coca-Cola are available, beer is the most popular draught. Most bars stock bottled brands, but in rural areas they may also offer traditional brews made locally from maize, bananas, pineapples or millet. East African men are famed for their thirst: on pay day, the bars are jammed all evening with carousers drinking steadily, exchanging jokes, and dancing to the juke box or a band.

Gaily decorated by self-taught artists, seven bars in Tanzania and Kenya (*left and above*) **attract customers with a wide range of advertising images, both modern and traditional—from wild animals to Mickey Mouse, and from village elders with drinking horns to smartly dressed professional couples.**

seven years of education behind him, Musa decided to make his fortune in the city, where his cousin had a job as a filing clerk. The cousin helped them build their first tiny shack in a valley near the centre, but whenever it rained the mud floor turned into slime, so they moved further out on to higher ground. Here they had more space and more air to breathe.

Finding a job proved depressingly difficult. Musa went from door to door looking for work, and asked everyone he knew for help, but without success. Relatives gave the family enough food to stay alive, but Musa began to fear that he would eventually be reduced to foraging around the rubbish tips: many people had already gone that way, abandoning hope entirely after years without any kind of work. Then his cousin helped them out again, recommending Musa when a post in his own company became free.

The messenger's job does not pay much, and Musa cannot afford to take one of the crowded buses or communal taxis that ply the routes into the city centre. He is constantly on his feet, walking six kilometres into the office, delivering letters and parcels all day, and walking home again at night. He is always tired. The family can only survive on his meagre earnings because they keep their spending to the absolute minimum. They wear their clothes almost until they fall off, and the children have never worn shoes; Musa's own pair have been patched and re-patched by the local cobbler.

Their diet is remorselessly plain: day after day, they eat nothing but plantain with a thin sauce made of dried beans and ground nuts mashed up with water. But every month or so, Musa manages to save just enough to catch the bus to his home village, to visit his parents. He helps tend the vegetable plots, and takes some food back to his family: a pumpkin and potatoes, perhaps even a chicken.

Musa's cousin earns little more than Musa, but he has only two children and his wife works as a nanny for a lawyer's family. They can afford to have meat regularly, as often as three or four times a week, and eat rice as well as maize flour, to say nothing of fish, manioc, plantain and other vegetables. Sometimes they even indulge in bottled beer and soft drinks like Coca-Cola. They buy their clothes from shops instead of shanty-town tailors, and even the children wear shoes. Sometimes the whole family visits the cinema, and occasionally the husband goes out for the evening to a dance hall. He has taken Musa with him once or twice, but the awareness of his own poverty depressed Musa so much that he took no pleasure in the trip.

Musa still hopes that the future will be brighter. If he can hold on to his present job, he might eventually become a filing clerk himself: then he could move out of the shanty town forever. His name is on the list for a flat on a housing estate, which admittedly is far from grand. The toilet is outside and the bathroom is a room with a bucket and drain. But the building has concrete walls and a corrugated-iron roof, and each flat comprises two small bedrooms, a living room and a tiny kitchen; there is electric light and cold running water.

Although the estate has flats of different sizes, and there are even some detached houses, they all have the same dull appearance. In the morning, when the workers leave, the place looks like an ant hill. Compared to Musa's

5

present home, however, it is a city of palaces. He knows he cannot compete with men of real education, perhaps 12 years of school and college, leading to diplomas and degrees: such people have their own houses, and might even drive cars. For Musa, a flat is the best he can hope for. It is on estates like these that the majority of townspeople live out their lives.

As East Africa looks forward to the 21st century, the most thoughtful of its leaders—whether politicians, teachers, writers or artists—are engaged in a fierce debate about their changing society. As they watch the new invade the ancient in myriad different ways, overturning hallowed traditions and upsetting old beliefs, some fear the loss of traditional heritage and predict a cultural crisis for East Africa. Others welcome the process of change. They remember the disunity of the past, and regard the eradication of tribal ways as an essential stage in the development of a modern society.

For politicians, the main challenge is to create a new national identity, and a grand opportunity arises whenever the so-called "gold caravan" of African heads of state descends on Nairobi, Kampala or Dar es Salaam for a meeting of the Organization of African Unity. This is an occasion for the leaders of each nation to show the outside world, through news film and press coverage, a carefully prepared image of their lands. The details may vary from country to country, but the common goal is to demonstrate a thoroughly modern blend of the best in African culture with the best the world has to offer.

Take, for example, a meeting in Nairobi. Dancers from all over the country arrive at Kenyatta Airport soon after dawn, ready to greet the delegates with the traditional dances of their region. Their eye-catching garments are not traditional, however; the dyed skirts and the brightly printed bodices are designed to entertain the tourists. Musicians wearing T-shirts—drummers, flautists, harpists and xylophonists, people who ring bells and hit wood and metal—set out their instruments and embark on an impromptu rehearsal. They are then joined by marching brass bands from the military, whose bright red uniforms and gleaming black boots—adopted from the British Army—are topped by a bearskin-style hat, which is in fact made from the black and white coat of the colobus monkey.

By the time the first plane arrives, everyone is in their allotted place. The chief of protocol is instructing his retinue, and the receiving ministers are all present and ready. The guard of honour stands stiffly on the tarmac, rifles held ready to present arms. As each delegation disembarks, the brass band plays its national anthem. After inspecting the guard of honour, the visitors walk towards the musicians and dancers, who fling themselves into a brief frenzy. Then the delegates make their way to the motorcade of gleaming Mercedes limousines which will deliver them to the city.

As the diplomats drive in a ceremonial convoy down Kenyatta Avenue, steering well clear of the shanty towns, television cameras record the scene, radio commentators speak breathlessly into microphones, while journalists scribble in notebooks. The tone is always loyal and respectful. In African newspapers the next day, the most daring editors may risk an occasional

In a shady square on Kenya's offshore island of Lamu, men in white Muslim caps shop for locally grown mangoes, coconuts and bananas. The goods are brought to market by donkey-drawn barrows—almost the only vehicles allowed on Lamu, where trucks and cars are prohibited.

5

tongue-in-cheek comment or print a photograph that shows a leader in an unflattering light; they even question whether the country can afford such extravaganzas. But the image East Africa wants to present to the world—the confidence and efficiency of the West laced with the distinctive traditions of Africa—will reach a wide audience at home and abroad. The dancers and drummers will get special prominence. As vital ingredients in the cultural mix, they are a declaration—like Kenyatta's celebrated fez and fly-whisk—that old values still survive, and are as cherished, at least in public, as the silk ties and Rolex watches that adorn the leaders' bodies.

The attention paid to such symbols may seem like lip-service to sceptical observers, but it touches a nerve in all East Africans. Peasants listening in remote villages to the radio broadcasts detect the music of their region and applaud the players, much as a villager in the Hebrides or the Alps is grateful to see a local celebrity on a nationwide television programme. Such an experience, however fleeting, strengthens the sense of community, of sharing in the life of the nation. And intellectuals living in the cities demand even more, not less, tradition, for among the educated Africans especially, there is a widespread acknowledgement that much has been lost during the journey into modern nationhood.

Since the first years of the Independence struggle, writers and artists have warned that the customs and beliefs of the past could not be abandoned without cost. Although they had evolved in the countryside, and were not easily adapted to life in the towns, they alone provided the individual with a clear moral outlook, as well as a sense of belonging to a wider community. Imported ideologies could never fill this gap, whether they were taken from the West or the East; there had to be an African solution, and this would mean building on the wisdom of the past.

For East Africans in the 1980s, this is proving a forbidding task. The European invasion, and the disparagement of tribal ways by both missionaries and teachers, seriously undermined their traditional way of life. Children may no longer be taught their ancestral myths, nor be instructed in the complex etiquette that many communities had developed; few undergo the training in moral conduct that used to accompany initiation. Consequently, much of the old knowledge has been lost forever, since most communities had no means of preserving their culture: they had no written language and few artistic traditions strong enough to survive in an era of change.

The Makonde of southern Tanzania carve ghosts and spirits reflecting the folklore and legends of their homeland, although most are now made specially for export. In Kenya, the Kamba still make drums and carve wooden stools; the Masai make elaborate and decorative beadwork. Otherwise, the culture of most East African communities consists of stories, songs and dances, many of which are rapidly dying out; they could be lost forever before the end of the century if a concerted effort is not launched to record them.

The education system may offer the best hope for the future, yet for several decades it was the biggest single threat to cultural survival. All three nations at Independence declared their aim to provide universal primary schooling on the Western model, and devoted up to 20 per cent of their budgets to this

In a mud-walled Protestant church in the countryside north of Kampala, a lay minister leads his congregation in Sunday prayer. Roughly two thirds of the Ugandan population are Christian, a higher proportion than in either of the two neighbouring lands.

KEEPING FAITH WITH ASIAN WAYS

Asians of the Jain religious sect watch a priest perform the sacraments at their temple in Mombasa.

Few communities in East Africa have preserved their cultural heritage as carefully as the Asians. Descendants of workers who arrived in the 1890s to build the Uganda railway and of the traders and peasants who followed, they still speak the old languages. The men have adopted European clothes, but Asian women still wear brightly coloured saris; and the Sikhs wear turbans and leave their hair uncut.

To outsiders, the Asians may seem a single, closed community, since they live in their own sections of the towns and rarely intermarry with Africans. But old divisions of religion and language split them into numerous smaller groups. The Punjabi-speakers may be Hindus, Muslims or Sikhs; the Gujaratis are mainly Hindus or adherents of the Jain religious sect; and the minority of Goans profess Christianity.

The Asians, who were given trading privileges by the British, came to dominate East African commerce in colonial times; but since Independence they have suffered from a backlash of African resentment. In 1972, Idi Amin expelled almost all the Ugandan community. Many Asians have since left Kenya and Tanzania too; by 1985, their numbers had dropped by more than half, to some 50,000 in Kenya and approximately 30,000 in Tanzania, though they remain a force in business.

5

task. By 1980, Kenya claimed that 95 per cent of all children between five and 12 were attending classes. Tanzania followed close behind, though Uganda's programme had already been seriously disrupted by years of civil war. In those first years, nearly all schools followed the syllabus first established by Britain.

Even in the 1980s, most of the history and literature taught in East African schools concerns Britain and other countries equally far away; and the few books available describing East Africa are mostly written by foreigners who, however sympathetic, inevitably take the outsider's point of view. Local knowledge, even about farming techniques, botany and zoology, is generally ignored, and children miss out on much useful information they would previously have learnt by word of mouth from relatives and friends.

Recently, however, there has been a shift of emphasis, so that in many of the schools the syllabus has been redirected towards the rural community. Pupils now have the opportunity to study farming methods, grow crops and raise livestock to sell in the market; they may also study local history, traditional crafts and customs, folklore and religious beliefs. Some schools avail themselves of the services of old people, either specialists in fields such as faiths, medicines, folklore, carving, singing and dancing, or just ordinary folk who have lived long enough and listened to the elders carefully enough to pass on in the oral tradition what things were like in the past.

Of the three countries, Tanzania has been the most committed to salvaging its own heritage. In his inaugural year as President, Nyerere set up a Ministry of National Culture. Later he was to claim that "of all the crimes of colonialism, there is none worse than the attempt to make us believe we had no culture of our own, or what we did have was worthless". He went on to protest about the decline in traditional dancing: "Many of us have learned to dance the rumba or the chachacha, to rock'n'roll or to twist. How many of us can dance, or have even heard of, the gombe sugu, the mangala, the konge or the lele mama?" University students were subsequently ordered to take traditional dance classes and Tanzania's quickly established National Dancing Troupe soon toured the country, learning and performing dances from all the regions, and developing new routines of their own.

Although Nyerere was eager to encourage traditional art forms, he was also wary of closing the door to foreign influences. "A nation which refuses to learn from foreign cultures," he warned, "is nothing but a nation of idiots and lunatics." The crucial concern was never to lose sight of the past. When the town bands of Dar es Salaam, which play in bars and at parties as well as weddings and funerals, picked up the influences of West Indian reggae, black American jazz and soul, Nigerian hi-life and even European rock, their music remained recognizably African. As in Kenya and Uganda, the new town music is performed regularly on radio and heard in villages all over the country.

In all three countries, the communications media rival education in their power to help form a new national culture—or to destroy what is left of the old. Independence and the transistor radio reached East Africa almost simultaneously, and by the mid-1970s nearly every village in the region had a radio. In the poorest areas, where few individuals could afford one, villagers clubbed together to buy a communal set. All the stations are controlled by government and present worthy accounts of national policies, local history and culture, but the most popular programmes play non-stop music. And with cheap cassette recorders ever more widely available, almost every bus and taxi blasts out music: villagers who just a few years ago heard only their local songs now face a steady barrage of African town music and the latest products of Los Angeles, New York or London, most frequently recorded on bootleg labels.

Television, also owned by the state, has been much slower to develop, because the production and transmission costs are so much higher than for radio. As a result, very few programmes are made locally. The wealthier inhabitants of Zanzibar, Nairobi, Kisumu, Kampala and other cities served by transmitters watch a nightly offering of national and international news, plus American and British shows such as *Dallas* and police thrillers like *The Sweeney*. Mainland Tanzania still had no TV station in the mid-1980s; the government declared that such imports were a threat to national culture, and pledged to wait until it could afford to make its own programmes.

Newspapers are equally dependent on overseas sources. The international news is supplied by major agencies like Reuters and Agence France Presse, while Kenyan and Ugandan newspapers also carry syndicated reports of British soccer and cricket matches, as well as international cartoon strips like *Snoopy*, *Hagar the Horrible* and *Andy Capp*. Kenyan journalists are allowed considerable freedom when reporting

Zanzibari children play football outside a block of flats reserved for civil servants. Housing is scarce in the cities, and such accommodation, providing electricity and cold running water, is a highly prized perquisite for state employees.

domestic affairs. They have caused resignations from the government, because of their investigations of several major scandals. Ugandan reporters have even greater latitude, although they were virtually silenced during the Amin years. But Tanzania's press is owned and paid for by the government; it eschews all frivolities. Writers may comment critically on the implementation of policies, but they do not criticize the policies themselves.

Because governments are so concerned to control the output of news, the press has little impact anywhere in the formation of a national culture; rather it reflects the political climate of each country. Circulations are low by international standards. In 1980, Tanzania's three national newspapers had a combined daily circulation of only 139,000; Uganda's nationals were hampered by shortages of newsprint, and collapsed disastrously from an Independence peak of 65,000 to a low of 25,000 in 1983; even Kenya's four national dailies sold only 259,000 copies a day that year. As the newspapers are printed and distributed mainly in the towns, and can be read only by the educated, they tend to widen the gap between town and country, prosperous and poor, however much their editors might like to reach a wider audience.

For Ngugi wa Thiongó, Kenya's best-known author, the widening gulf between the élite and the masses is a political as well as cultural problem. In his view, the prosperous and educated Africans of the cities are in danger of becoming mere "black Europeans", with attitudes and lifestyles indistinguishable from the colonials whose places in society they have taken. His most famous work, *Petals of Blood*, contrasted the hardships faced by Kenyan peasants with the luxuries enjoyed by the corrupt and wealthy. The novel was a bestseller in East Africa, but because it was written in English and had little effect on the villagers it championed, the government did not suppress it. When Ngugi wrote a similarly radical play, *Ngaahika Ndeenda* (*I*

5

A Kenyan golfer putts towards the flag at Mombasa Golf Club, on the shores of the Indian Ocean. Africans have adopted many European sports, including squash and tennis; in 1968, five years after Independence, a Kenyan African won the national amateur golf title for the first time.

Will Marry When I Like), in Kikuyu and then attempted to stage it in a Kikuyu village with ordinary peasants and workers as the actors, he was jailed for a year without trial, and later went into exile in London.

Two Ugandan writers, Okot p'Bitek and Robert Serumaga, took less aggressive stances, but both struggled with the underlying problems of taking art to the people. Okot p'Bitek's *Song of Lawino*, written in the form of a traditional song, was composed originally in his own Acholi language before he translated it into English. But the choice of a local language, even if it does bridge town and country, also means that an author's potential readership is reduced. Robert Serumaga's theatre company, Abafumi, attempted to blend music, dance and drama together so that the meaning of their works would exist independently of the written word. Their performances were acclaimed not only in Uganda, but all over Africa, as well as by international audiences on tours in Europe and the United States.

Painters also encounter difficulties in finding appreciation, because there are very few public galleries, and opportunites for exhibiting their work are rare. But two artists from Tanzania, Elimo Najau and Sam Ntiro, have attempted to fuse traditional themes and techniques with modern idioms. Elimo Njau's most famous works are the murals at the Muranga (Fort Hall) Memorial Chapel in Kenya, which is devoted to the victims of the Emergency; Sam Ntiro, whose studio at Mount Kilimanjaro lies in the heart of the Chagga region, has painted religious scenes set in an African landscape. Since both trained at Uganda's Makerere Art College and later worked in Kenya, they have influenced many of the region's younger artists.

As East Africa's élite of politicians, teachers, musicians and artists grapple with the task of creating a cultural identity, the athletes of the region have stirred deep national pride with their achievements at the Olympic Games. These men are the heroes who have replaced the great warriors of the past as representatives of the community, whose achievements are pure and direct, unsullied by social grievance or political controversy. Peasants in the Mountains of the Moon rejoiced with fishermen on the Indian Ocean when the radio reported that Kenya's Kip Keino had raced to win a gold medal for the 1,500 metres at the Mexico Olympics of 1968; they cheered again when he took the steeplechase gold at Munich in 1972, where Uganda's John Akii Bua won the 400-metres hurdle.

The lucky few who watched these events on television in Nairobi or in Kampala experienced the same elation at seeing an East African salute from the podium as the national flag rose behind him. Such moments are all the sweeter for their rarity; and the incontrovertible evidence that East Africans can hold their own against all comers plays a crucial part in building confident national cultures. Seen in this light, the applause of the crowds when an athlete triumphs or when a cavalcade of politicians sweeps through the capital is no empty gesture. For Dr. Paul, in his Nairobi mansion, as for Musa in the shanty town, these self-made men at the height of their powers are living proof that life can get better, that talents and hard work can be rewarded. And in new nations, only now entering their second generation, the spirit of optimism still burns bright.

CAMEL-HERDERS OF THE WILDERNESS

Photographs by Amos Schliack

In the stony wilderness of north-central Kenya, where meagre rains fall only in spring and summer, some 20,000 Rendille tribesmen lead an ancient lifestyle almost untouched by the modern world. Herds of camels, goats and sheep provide their sustenance; acacia and wild sisal supply materials for their homes; and for their few luxuries, such as cloth and jewellery, they barter with wandering traders.

The married men, women and young children live in fenced settlements, near wells dug in river beds; they keep sheep and goats, and a few milking camels. But grazing is scarce; so unmarried Rendille men and boys must travel ceaselessly with the rest of the camels, living in makeshift camps while they scour the barren land for grass and shrubs to serve as pasture. The herds may number as many as 1,000 beasts, each capable of travelling for up to a fortnight without water; the men who guard them survive by drinking their milk or if necessary by tapping their veins for blood.

Bending under a load of acacia branches gathered for firewood, a Rendille girl chews nonchalantly on a twig as she heads for home. Most girls are married by the age of 14; as indicated by her necklace of white beads, this girl is still single.

Spear in hand, a young herdsman chases a stray camel through bushes green after the rains. Although they may travel as many as 40 kilometres a day in search of pasture, the Rendille never ride their camels.

While her baby watches inquisitively, a Rendille woman ties a sisal mat to a framework of acacia branches in the course of constructing a sleeping hut. When drought or depleted grazing force her clan to relocate their settlement, the hut will be taken down and the matting saved for re-use.

A thorny stockade surrounds a small Rendille settlement of about 30 huts. Each family has a byre for its goats, sheep and a few milking camels.

Elaborate jewellery made from glass, metal or even plastic marks an individual's status in Rendille society. Married women wear necklaces made of beads and copper wire and elaborate headbands *(below and bottom left)*; married men are identified by large, circular earrings *(bottom right)*.

Shortly before his marriage, a bridegroom squats patiently while a friend dyes his hair red with an ochre paste, made by mixing earth and camel urine. The wedding celebrations—a festive occasion for dancing and feasting—will last for eight days.

Herds of goats and sheep surround a watering hole. The women with them will take water back to their settlement in containers carried by the camels.

ACKNOWLEDGEMENTS

The index for this book was prepared by Vicki Robinson. For their help in the preparation of this volume, the editors wish to thank: Terry Barringer, Royal Commonwealth Society, London; Mark Boulton, International Centre for Conservation Education, Gloucester, England; Mike Brown, London; Nicos and Louise Caratsis, Nairobi; Chris Ellwood, Botany Library, Natural History Museum, London; Helen Grubin, London; Richard Hall, The Observer, London; Ken James, Unilever Plc, London; Craig Johnson, World Wildlife Fund, Godalming, Surrey, England; Kenya High Commission, London; Uli Malisius, Department of Land and Surveys, Zanzibar; Marek Mayer, Environmental Data Services, London; Hezbon Mbori, Asat Fishermen's Co-operative, Kisumu, Kenya; Patrick Mulvarney, Intermediate Technology Development Group, Rugby, England; Mr. S. J. Musandu, Ministry of Information and Broadcasting, Nairobi; Mr. A. Musumba, Kenya Railways, Nairobi; Anton Neumann, London; Joseph Ngala and Fr. Arnold Grol, Kenya Catholic Secretariat, Nairobi; David Omolo, Kenya Railways, Fort Ternan, Kenya; Elizabeth Plint, London; Pierre Portas, World Conservation Centre, Geneva; Arnold Raphael, Zimbabwe Newspapers Ltd., London; Abdulla Riyami, Dar es Salaam; Sally Rowland, Saffron Walden, Essex, England; John Stoneman, Overseas Development Association, London; Hafidh Ali Tahir, Zanzibar; Tanzania High Commission, London; Jo Taylor, Conservation Monitoring Centre, Cambridge, England; Deborah Thompson, London; Lloyd Timberlake, Earthscan, London; Ann Turner, Nairobi; Richard Widdows, Suffolk, England.

PICTURE CREDITS

Credits from left to right are separated by semicolons, from top to bottom by dashes.

Cover: Brian Boyd from Colorific!, London. Front endpaper: Map by Roger Stewart, London. Back endpaper: Digitized image by Ralph Scott/ Chapman Bounford, London.

1, 2: © Flag Research Center, Winchester, Massachusetts. **6–13**: Christopher Pillitz, London. (Digitized images by Ralph Scott/ Chapman Bounford, London). **14, 15**: Peter Davey from Bruce Coleman Ltd., Uxbridge, England. **16, 17**: Robert Caputo, Washington, D.C. **19**: John Cleare. **20**: Caroline Weaver from Ardea Photographics, London; John Moss from Colorific!, London—Victor Lamont from The Hutchison Library, London; Liba Taylor from The Hutchison Library, London—Mohamed Amin from Camerapix Picture Library, London; David Keith Jones, Lichfield, Staffordshire, England–John Moss from Colorific!, London; Robert Caputo, Washington, D.C.; John Shaw from Bruce Coleman Ltd., Uxbridge, England; Mohamed Amin from Camerapix Picture Library, London (2). (Digitized image by Ralph Scott/Chapman Bounford, London). **22**: Gunter Ziesler from Bruce Coleman Ltd., Uxbridge, England. **23**: Alexander Lindsay from The Hutchison Library, London. **24**: Ian Beames from Ardea Photographics, London. **25**: Mike Price from Survival Anglia Ltd., London. **26, 27**: Gunter Ziesler from Bruce Coleman Ltd., Uxbridge, England. **28**: David Keith Jones, Lichfield, Staffordshire, England. **30, 31**: Christopher Pillitz, London. **32, 33**: Jean Valentin from Explorer, Paris. **35**: Robert Caputo, Washington, D.C. **36**: Nick Owen from The Hutchison Library, London. **37**: The Hutchison Library, London. **38, 39**: Robert Caputo, Washington, D.C. **40, 41**: Mohamed Amin from Camerapix Picture Library, London. **42, 43**: Ian Beames from Ardea Photographics, London. **44**: Leo Dickinson from Daily Telegraph Colour Library, London. **45–47**: Robert Caputo, Washington, D.C. **48**: *Cantino* map courtesy of Biblioteca Estense, Modena, Italy, photo David Lees, Florence. **50**: Courtesy of Museum of Mankind, London. **51**: Mohamed Amin from Camerapix Picture Library, London. **52**: Murray Cards (International) Ltd., London. **53**: Digitized image by Ralph Scott/Chapman Bounford, London. **55**: Courtesy of The United Society for the Propagation of the Gospel, London. **56**: Map by Roger Stewart, London; courtesy of The Royal Commonwealth Society, London. **57**: Courtesy of The Royal Commonwealth Society, London. **60**: *Mombasa* from *Livro do Estado India Oriental*, MS Sloane 197f 103v104 courtesy of The British Library, London—courtesy of London Borough Council, Richmond upon Thames; courtesy of Museum of Mankind, London. **61**: Courtesy of Imperial War Museum, London; Felix Greene from The Hutchison Library, London—Associated Press Ltd., London. **62, 63**: Courtesy of The Royal Commonwealth Society, London. **64, 65**: Courtesy of Imperial War Museum, London. **66**: Digitized images by Ralph Scott/Chapman Bounford, London. **68**: The Hutchison Library, London. **70, 71**: Baron Hugo van Lawick, London (inset: The Photo Source, London). **73**: Courtesy of Imperial War Museum, London. **74–81**: Christopher Pillitz, London. Digitized image by Ralph Scott/Chapman Bounford, London). **82**: William Campbell/ SYGMA from The John Hillelson Picture Agency, London; Camerapix Picture Library, London. **83**: Camerapix Picture Library, London. **84, 85**: Camera Press Ltd., London. **87, 88**: Terence Spencer, London. **89**: Popperfoto, London. **90, 91**: Camera Press Ltd., London. **93**: Courtesy of The Royal Commonwealth Society, London. **94**: BBC Hulton Picture Library, London. **96, 98**: Camera Press Ltd., London. **101**: Jean Pierre Laffont/SYGMA from The John Hillelson Picture Agency, London. **102–109**: Christopher Pillitz, London. **110**: Robert Caputo, Washington, D.C. **113**: Peter Carmichael from Aspect Picture Library, London. **114, 115**: Georg Fischer from Visum, Hamburg. **116, 117**: Christopher Pillitz, London. **119**: David Keith Jones, Lichfield, Staffordshire, England. **120–122**: Christopher Pillitz, London. **123**: Victoria Southwell from The Hutchison Library, London. **124**: Patricio Goycolea from The Hutchison Library, London. **125**: Dr. Georg Gerster from The John Hillelson Picture Agency, London. **126**: Courtesy of the British Museum (Natural History), London; Mohamed Amin from Camerapix Picture Library, London. **128, 129**: Dr. Georg Gerster from The John Hillelson Picture Agency, London. **130, 131**: Robert Caputo, Washington, D.C. **132, 133**: Christopher Pillitz, London. **135**: John Hopewell from RIDA Photo Library, London. **136**: Elisabeth Boulton from International Centre for Conservation Education, Guiting Power, Gloucestershire, England. **138**: Christopher Pillitz, London; Peter Carmichael from Aspect Picture Library, London—David Keith Jones, Lichfield, Staffordshire, England (2)—Mark Saunders from The Hutchison Library, London; Peter Carmichael from Aspect Picture Library, London. **139–141**: Christopher Pillitz, London. **142**: Chris Steele-Perkins/Magnum Distribution from The John Hillelson Picture Agency, London. **143, 145**: Christopher Pillitz, London. **146, 147**: Liba Taylor from The Hutchison Library, London. **148–151**: Amos Schliack from Focus, Hamburg. **152**: Amos Schliack from Focus, Hamburg—Amos Schliack from Agence ANA, Paris. **153**: Amos Schliack from Agence ANA, Paris. **154, 155**: Amos Schliack from Focus, Hamburg

BIBLIOGRAPHY

BOOKS

Africa Review. World of Information, Saffron Walden, Essex.

Allen, Charles, ed., *Tales from the Dark Continent*. André Deutsch, London, 1979.

Amin, Mohamed, *Journey through Tanzania*. The Bodley Head, London, 1984.

Arnold, Guy, *Modern Kenya*. Longman Group, Essex, 1981.

Attwood, William, *The Reds and the Blacks*. Hutchinson, London, 1967.

Avirgan, T. and Honey, M., *War in Uganda*. Zed Press, London, 1982.

Barnett, Donald L., and Njama, Karavi, *Mau Mau from Within*. Macgibbon and Kee, London, 1966.

Bennett, G., *Kenya: The Colonial Period*. Oxford University Press, 1963.

Best, Nicholas, *Happy Valley*. Secker & Warburg, London, 1979.

Casimati, Nina, *Guide to East Africa, Kenya, Tanzania & the Seychelles*. Travelaid, London, 1985.

Coulson, Andrew, *Tanzania, A Political Economy*. Clarendon Press, Oxford, 1982.

Davidson, Basil, *Africa in Modern History*. Penguin Books, London, 1978.

Davidson, Basil, *Black Mother: Africa and the Atlantic Slave Trade*. Penguin Books, London, 1980.

Denyer, Susan, *African Traditional Architecture*. Heinemann, London, 1978.

Dorst, Jean, and Dandelot, Pierre, *A Field Guide to the Larger Mammals of Africa*. Collins, London, 1970.

Evans, P., *Law and Disorder: Scenes of Life in Kenya*. Secker & Warburg, London, 1956.

Fagg, William, and Picton, John, *The Potter's Art in Africa*. British Museum Publications, London, 1978.

Farrant, Leda, *The Legendary Grogan*. Hamish Hamilton, London, 1981.

Fox, James, *White Mischief*. Jonathan Cape, London, 1982.

Freund, Bill, *The Making of Contemporary Africa*. Macmillan, London, 1984.

Gingyera-Pinycwa, A.G.G., *Apollo Milton Obote and His Times*. NOK Publishers International, New York, 1978.

Grahame, Iain, *Amin and Uganda*. Granada Publishing, London, 1980.

Harlow, Vincent, and Chilver, E.M., eds., *History of East Africa*, Volume II. Oxford University Press, 1965.

Hatch, John, *Tanzania, A Profile*. Pall Mall Press, London, 1972.

Hatch, John, *Two African Statesmen*. Secker & Warburg, London, 1976.

Huntingford, G.W.B., *The Southern Nilo-Hamites*. International African Institute, London, 1969.

Huxley, Elspeth, *The Flame Trees of Thika*. Penguin Books, London, 1962.

Huxley, Elspeth, *White Man's Country*. Chatto and Windus, London, 1935.

Ibingira, Grace, *African Upheavals since Independence*. Westview Press, Colorado, 1981.

Iliffe, John, *A Modern History of Tanganyika*. Cambridge University Press, 1979.

Iliffe, John, *Tanganyika Under German Rule*. Cambridge University Press, 1969.

Ingham, K., *The Making of Modern Uganda*. George Allen & Unwin, London, 1958.

Jørgensen, J.J., *Uganda: A Modern History*. Croom Helm, Beckenham, Kent, 1980.

Kaplan, Irving, ed., *Tanzania, A Country Study*. The American University, Washington, 1978.

Karugire, Samwiri Rubaraza, *A Political History of Uganda*. Heinemann

Educational Books, Nairobi, 1980.

Kayongo-Male, Diane, and Onyango, Philista, *The Sociology of the African Family*. Longman Group, Essex, 1984.

Keith Jones, David, *Shepherds of the Desert*. Elm Tree Books, London, 1984.

Kenya Churches Handbook. Evangel Publishing House, Kisumu, Kenya, 1973.

Kenyatta, Jomo, *Facing Mount Kenya*. Heinemann, London, 1979.

Kesby, John D., *The Cultural Regions of East Africa*. Academic Press, London, 1977.

Krapf, J.L., *Travels, Researches and Missionary Labours During an Eighteen Years' Residence in Eastern Africa*. Trübner, London, 1860.

Kyemba, Henry, *State of Blood*. Corgi Books, London, 1977.

Leakey, Mary, *Africa's Vanishing Art*. Hamish Hamilton, London, 1983.

Leakey, L.S.B., *Kenya, Contrasts and Problems*. Methuen, London, 1936.

Liebenow, J. Gus, *Colonial Rule and Political Development in Tanzania: The Case of the Makonde*. East African Publishing House, Nairobi, 1971.

Low, D.A., and Smith, Alison, eds., *History of East Africa*, Volume III. Oxford University Press, 1976.

Mamdani, M., *Imperialism and Fascism in Uganda*. Heinemann, London, 1983.

Martin, Esmond, *Zanzibar: Tradition and Revolution*. Hamish Hamilton, London, 1978.

Matthiessen, Peter, *The Tree Where Man Was Born*. Pan Books, London, 1984.

Mboya, T.J., *The Kenya Question*. Fabian Colonial Bureau, London, 1956.

Meredith, Martin, *The First Dance of Freedom*. Hamish Hamilton, London, 1984.

Meinertzhagen, Richard, *Army Diary, 1899–1926*. Oliver and Boyd, London, 1960.

Meinertzhagen, Richard, *Kenya Diary, 1902–1906*. Eland Books, London, 1983.

Middleton, John, and Campbell, J., *Zanzibar: Its Politics and Its Society*. Oxford University Press, 1965.

Middleton, John and Kershaw, Greet, *The Kikuyu and Kamba of Kenya*. International African Institute, London, 1972.

Miller, Charles, *The Lunatic Express*. Macmillan, London, 1971.

Miller, Norman, *Kenya: the Quest for Prosperity*. Gower Publishing, Aldershot, Hampshire, 1984.

Mitchell, Sir P., *African Afterthoughts*. Hutchinson, London, 1954.

Moorehead, Alan, *The White Nile*. Penguin Books, London, 1973.

Morgan, W.T.W., *East Africa*. Longman Group, Essex, 1973.

Morgan, W.T.W., *Nairobi: City and Region*. Oxford University Press, 1967.

Mosley, Leonard, *Duel for Kilimanjaro*. Weidenfeld and Nicolson, London, 1963.

Mungeam, G.H., *British Rule in Kenya*. Clarendon Press, Oxford, 1966.

Murray, Jocelyn, ed., *Cultural Atlas of Africa*. Phaidon Press, Oxford, 1981.

Murray-Brown, Jeremy, *Kenyatta*. George Allen & Unwin, London, 1972.

Mytton, Graham, *Mass Communication in Africa*. Edward Arnold, London, 1983.

Nelson, Harold D., ed., *Kenya, A Country Study*. The American University, Washington, 1984.

Ngugi, Wa Thiongo, *Devil on the Cross*. Heinemann, London, 1982.

Ngugi, Wa Thiongo, *Petals of Blood*. Heinemann, London, 1977.

Nicholls, C.S., *The Swahili Coast*. George Allen & Unwin, London, 1971.

Nyerere, Julius K., *Freedom and Unity*. Oxford University Press, Dar es Salaam/Oxford, 1966.

Nyerere, Julius K., *Ujamaa*. Oxford University Press, 1968.

O'Connor, Anthony, *The African City*. Hutchinson, London, 1983.

O'Connor, Anthony, *An Economic Geography of East Africa*. Bell & Sons, London, 1966.

Odinga, Oginga, *Not Yet Uhuru*. Heinemann, London, 1967.

Oliver, Roland, and Crowder, Michael, eds., *The Cambridge Encyclopaedia of Africa*. Cambridge University Press, 1981.

Oliver, Roland, and Matthew, Gervase, eds., *History of East Africa*, Volume I. Oxford University Press, 1963.

Patterson, J.H., *The Man-Eaters of Tsavo*. Macmillan, London, 1947.

Perrin Jassy, Marie-France, *Basic Community in the African Churches*. Orbis Books, New York, 1973.

Pratt, R.C., *The Critical Phase in Tanzania, 1945–1968*. Cambridge University Press, 1976.

Roberts, John, *A Land Full of People*. Eyre & Spottiswoode, London, 1967.

Robertson, A.F., *Community of Strangers*. Scolar Press, London, 1978.

Roosevelt, Theodore, *African Game Trails*. Scribner, New York, 1910.

Ross, Marc Howard, *Grass Roots in an African City*. Massachusetts Institute of Technology Press, Cambridge, Massachusetts, 1975.

Shorter, Aylward, *East African Societies*. Routledge and Kegan Paul, London, 1974.

Smith, George Ivan, *Ghosts of Kampala*. Weidenfeld and Nicolson, London, 1980.

Speke, John Hanning, *Journal of the Discovery of the Source of the Nile*. William Blackwood and Sons, London, 1863.

Spencer, Paul, *Nomads in Alliance*. Oxford University Press, 1973.

Thomson, Joseph, *Through Masai Land*. Houghton Mifflin, Boston, 1885.

Tosh, John, *Clan Leaders and Colonial Chiefs in Lango*. Oxford University Press, 1978.

Uzoigwe, G.N., ed., *Uganda: The Dilemma of Nationhood*. NOK Publishers

International, New York, 1982.

Walker, Eric, *Treetops Hotel*. Robert Hale, London, 1962.

Willett, Frank, *African Art*. Thames and Hudson, London, 1971.

Yeager, Rodger, *Tanzania, An African Experiment*. Gower Publishing, Aldershot, Hampshire, 1982.

PERIODICALS

British Empire series, Time-Life Books:
"Black Ivory", No. 4,
"Livingstone and Stanley", No. 26,
"Light in the Darkness", No. 27,
"The Source of the Nile", No. 37,
"Takeover in East Africa", No. 39,
"The Empire at War", No. 66,
"The Imperial Façade", No. 73,
"Uhuru for Kenya", No. 86.

George, Uwe, "An Ocean is Born", *GEO*, Collector's Edition, 1980.

Hall, Richard, "Stanley's Boldest Journey", *Observer*, October 6, 1974.

Kambites, Jerry and Sarah, "Return to Uganda", *National Geographic*, November 1985.

Kuenkel, Reinhard, "Cheetahs—Swift Cats of the Serengeti", *GEO*, Collector's Edition, 1980.

Minority Rights Group reports:
"The Asian Minorities of East and Central Africa", No. 4, April 1971.
"The New Position of East Africa's Asians", No. 16, November 1984.
"Uganda and Sudan", No. 66, December 1984.

"Uganda", *Amnesty International*, June 1985.

Weaver, Kenneth F., "The Search for Our Ancestors", *National Geographic*, November 1985.

World Bank reports:
"Accelerated Development in Sub-Saharan Africa, 1981."
"Kenya Population and Development, 1980."
"Toward Sustained Development in Sub-Saharan Africa, 1984."
"Uganda Country Economic Memorandum, 1982."

INDEX

Page numbers in italics refer to illustrations or illustrated text.

Colour separations by Fotolitomec, S.N.C., Milan, Italy.
Typesetting by Tradespools Ltd., Somerset, England.
Printed and bound by Artes Gráficas Toledo, S.A., Spain.
D. L. TO:1432 -1986

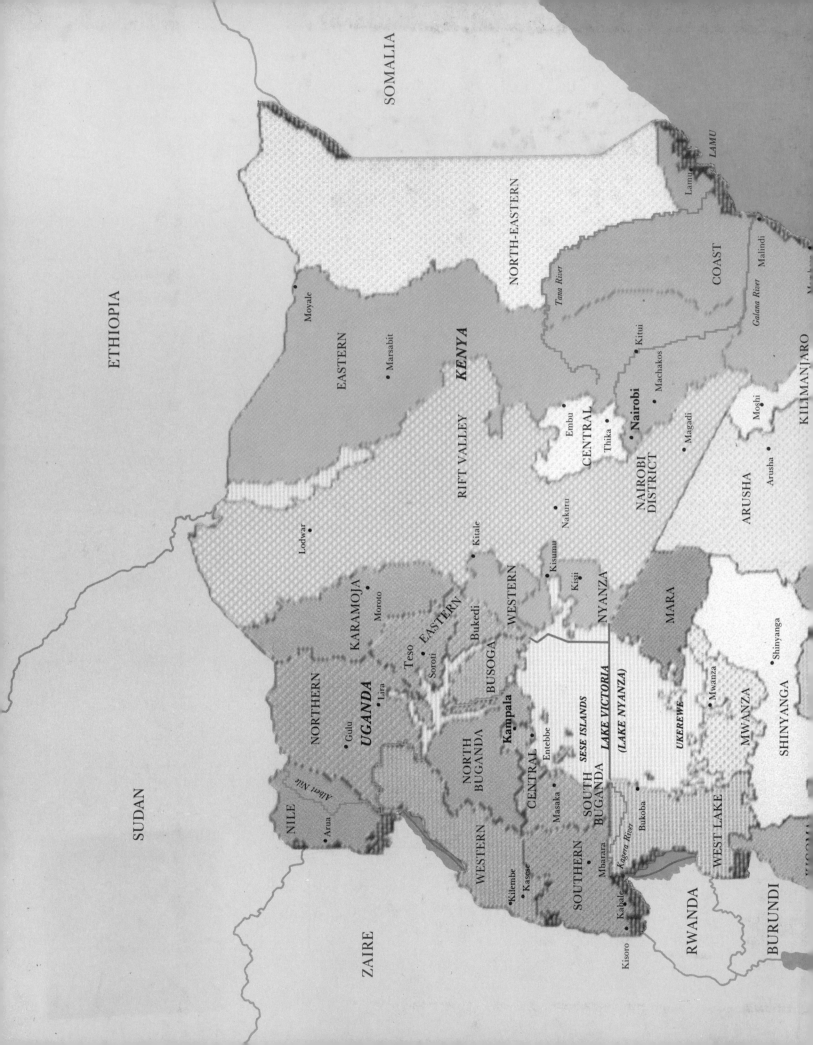